THE SYNOPTIC GOSPELS

by the same author

★

LANDMARKS IN THE STORY OF CHRISTIANITY
THE LIFE OF CHRIST
THE STUDY OF THE GOSPELS
THE ACTS OF THE APOSTLES
A CRITICAL INTRODUCTION TO THE GOSPELS
WHO'S WHO IN THE GOSPELS
THE GOSPEL OF MATTHEW
THE GOSPEL OF MARK
THE CHURCH IN THE NEW TESTAMENT
THE GOSPEL OF LUKE
THE FOURTH GOSPEL

THE SYNOPTIC GOSPELS

by

H. A. GUY, B.D., B.A.

Macmillan Education

© H. A. Guy 1960

All rights reserved. No reproduction, copy or transmission
of this publication may be made without written permission.

No paragraph of this publication may be reproduced, copied or
transmitted save with written permission or in accordance with
the provisions of the Copyright, Designs and Patents Act 1988,
or under the terms of any licence permitting limited copying
issued by the Copyright Licensing Agency, 33–4 Alfred Place,
London WC1E 7DP.

Any person who does any unauthorised act in relation to
this publication may be liable to criminal prosecution and
civil claims for damages.

First edition 1960

Published by
MACMILLAN EDUCATION LTD
Houndmills, Basingstoke, Hampshire RG21 2XS
and London
Companies and representatives
throughout the world

Printed in Hong Kong

ISBN 0–333–05081–9

22	24	26	28	30	29	27	25	23	21
92	94	96	98	00	99	97	95	93	91

PREFACE

THIS book is intended for those who wish not only to read the Gospels but to make an intelligent study of their contents. The reader will find here a summary and discussion of the views of modern scholars. It is hoped that this will assist him to understand the nature of the Synoptic Gospels and to appreciate their contents and message. It may also help to dispel some of the ignorance which is rife — among both those who accept and those who reject the Christian message — about the origins and character of the Gospels and their relations to each other.

Candidates for examinations, whose syllabus confines them to the first three Gospels, have been particularly in the author's mind. They should read thoroughly and carefully, mastering each point as it is dealt with, preferably making their own summary of the argument or discussion. They should look up every reference which is made to the Gospels. There are far too many people — including examination candidates at all levels — who are able to talk in general terms about the Gospels or dogmatise about their contents or argue vehemently for a particular point of view, but cannot support what they say by references or quotations from the books themselves. A book such as this is only a guide; it is not intended to be a substitute for study of the Gospels themselves.

It is assumed throughout that the reader will use the Revised Version (1881) or the Revised Standard

Version (1946); the latter has the accuracy of the former, with the advantage of dispensing with the archaisms which the Revised Version still retained. Both these translations are greatly superior to the 'Authorised' Version of 1611, for purity of text, accuracy and fidelity to the original writings. Translations by individuals such as R. F. Weymouth, J. Moffatt and E. V. Rieu are often helpful in illuminating passages which present difficulties in the more conventional renderings.

All students of the New Testament will greatly profit from using the translation published in 1961 under the title of The New English Bible.

H.A.G.

CONTENTS

Chapter		Page
	Preface	v
I.	Before the Gospels	1
II.	The Background of the Life of Jesus	14
III.	The Life of Jesus in the Synoptic Gospels	25
IV.	The First Written Gospel	43
V.	The Gospel of Mark	62
VI.	The Non-Markan Material in Matthew and Luke	82
VII.	The Characteristics of the Teaching of Jesus	98
VIII.	The Gospel of Matthew	110
IX.	The Gospel of Luke	123
X.	Jesus' Teaching about Man	135
XI.	'God and His Messiah'	151
XII.	The Kingdom of God and the Son of Man	164
	Books for Further Reading and Study	179
	Index of Subjects	181

CHAPTER I

BEFORE THE GOSPELS

BEFORE the Gospels there was a gospel. This somewhat paradoxical statement illustrates the two uses of the term by which we speak of the first four books of the New Testament. The English word 'gospel' comes from two Anglo-Saxon words, *god* and *spel*, meaning 'good story'. It was used to translate the Greek word *euaggelion*, which, through the Latin *evangelium*, has come into our language in such words as 'evangelist' and 'evangelical'.

The Christian gospel was originally a message which was spoken, not written down. Using the related verb, Luke characterises the announcement of the birth of Jesus as bringing 'good tidings of great joy' (Luke 2: 10). Paul uses the term in speaking of his own message — 'the gospel which I preach' (Gal. 2: 2). He calls this 'my gospel' (Rom. 2: 16; 16: 25) and refers to the gospel which was proclaimed by those also who were associated with him in the Christian mission (1 Thess. 1: 5; 2 Cor. 4: 3). The word is used in this sense in Mark 1: 14–15, where the writer says that Jesus 'came into Galilee, preaching the gospel of God', that the Kingdom of God was at hand. The 'heading' to this book combines both these senses — the good news preached by Jesus and the good news about Jesus — 'the beginning of the gospel of Jesus Christ' (Mark 1: 1).

We can see from a study of the speeches which are recorded in the Acts of the Apostles, and also from Paul's letters, what the early Christian gospel was. It centred in the proclamation of the coming of Jesus. History, the preachers declared, led up to that (and since history to them meant the story of the Hebrews, they naturally turned to the Old Testament for confirmation and illustration); a new era of history began with him (this meant for them that the Messianic age was a present reality); and the era would be closed with his triumph (which they sometimes pictured in terms borrowed from Jewish apocalyptic). The proclamation therefore would inevitably include some account of the coming of Jesus, his life, his teaching, his death and resurrection. It may seem at first that there is little reference to this in Paul's letters, but this is because he is not giving his teaching to his converts for the first time. He is advising them on practical or theological problems, which they themselves have often raised, and reminding them of the things which they should have already known. In the speeches in the Acts, by Peter, Paul and others, brief reference is made to the life and work of Jesus, especially when those who were being addressed had not had the opportunity of seeing him for themselves or were possibly hearing about him for the first time, as at Caesarea when Peter addressed Cornelius and his household (Acts 10: 36–43). The speeches in the Acts are only summaries of what was said and Peter's address was no doubt much longer than this and probably included some detailed information about the life of Jesus.

But the story of Jesus, as part of the proclamation of the good news and as a necessary part of the instruction of would-be members of the Church, was not written down at once. It was passed on by word of mouth. So the opening sentence of this chapter might read: 'Before the Gospels were written, there was a gospel which was told.'

There are three main reasons why the narrative was not immediately committed to writing:

(i) The early Christians were not literary people or folk with a great amount of leisure. Paul reminded his converts that their ranks included 'not many wise after the flesh, not many mighty, not many noble' (1 Cor. 1 : 26) — as this world viewed them — and most of the Christians of the first century would not have the ability or the time to set out a written account. Writing a book was a long and expensive business, as it had to be set down by hand on sheets of papyrus or a roll. Very few people could afford to possess books of their own. The members of a typical Jewish household in the time of Jesus, for instance, would not have a Bible of their own. If they wished to refer to a passage from the Old Testament, they would have to go to the synagogue and consult the Rabbi. The early Christians, most of them busy working people and many of them slaves, were not people accustomed to handling or writing books.

(ii) The Christians were too busy proclaiming their message and living it to bother about its permanent preservation. The urgent matter for them was for everyone to hear the gospel. This was the more important in view of their expectation that the 'end of the age' would soon come. They thought that Christ himself would reappear in glory and would bring the resurrection and judgment of men, ushering in a new age in which the Kingdom of God would have fully come. Paul himself thought, at one time in his life at any rate, that his own generation would be the last — 'we that are alive, that are left for the coming of the Lord . . .' (1 Thess. 4: 15). Men must be told the message at once, before it was too late. As this 'consummation of the age' was so near, there would be no point in writing down accounts for the benefit of future generations.

(iii) The story would be remembered, without being written down. The people in the ancient world had extraordinary powers of memory. This is still the case in the east and in other places where people do not rely on the written word as we do. Among the Jews, the Rabbis used to instruct their pupils orally; their teaching was learned by heart, without any written notes. Jesus himself probably adopted this method in instructing his own disciples. They in turn would pass on his teaching and would tell of incidents at which they themselves had been present; their hearers would remember them and be able to relate them to others. In the Christian meetings, the stories of Jesus and his teaching would be repeated, to encourage church-members. They would also be included in the instruction given to converts. Missionaries would relate them in their preaching.

FORM CRITICISM

This 'oral period', before the completion of a written Gospel, lasted about a generation. During this time the tradition was necessarily fragmentary. Nobody would remember the whole of the story, as one connected account such as appears in our Gospels, and it would not be related as a whole. Separate incidents and passages of Jesus' teaching would be remembered by different individuals. As these were repeated, there would be a tendency for the stories to assume something like a regular form or pattern. We can still see traces of this in the written Gospels, for the narratives there can be classified in different types. Some of them have their chief interest in a statement by Jesus, some are stories of healing or other wonders, while others are about the companions of Jesus.

Much study has been given to this subject during the past thirty years and scholars have been examining and classifying the oral 'forms' which are still discernible in the written accounts. This study is called Form Criticism (or Form History; German *Formgeschichte*, for the Germans were the pioneers in this branch of New Testament criticism).[1] According to the Form Critics, we are able to place the material found in our Gospels into roughly four categories, corresponding to four types of oral material which were in circulation in the first generation of the early Church.

(i) Pronouncement-Stories (Vincent Taylor's term), or Paradigms (models — Martin Dibelius' term). These are stories which are linked with some saying of Jesus, with which the account concludes. Many of the short narratives in the Gospels seem to have their climax in a statement of Jesus. A clear instance is the story of the question about tribute money (Mark 12: 13–17):

'And they sent to him some of the Pharisees and

---

[1] Criticism here does not mean fault-finding, as it does so often in the popular use of the word. It is the scientific study of a subject by one who is qualified to be a critic or judge (Greek: *krites*). Such criticism is often appreciation rather than censure. Form Criticism is one branch of such study of the Gospels. Other branches are Textual Criticism (the study of the 'text' of a book, in manuscripts and translations, with a view to arriving at the original words of the author) and Source Criticism (the investigation of the sources or material which the author used in his work).

some of the Herodians, to entrap him in his talk. And they came and said to him, "Teacher, we know that you are true and care for no man; for you do not regard the position of men, but truly teach the way of God. Is it lawful to pay taxes to Caesar, or not? Should we pay them, or should we not?" But, knowing their hypocrisy, he said to them, "Why put me to the test? Bring me a coin, and let me look at it." And they brought one. And he said to them, "Whose likeness and inscription is this?" They said to him, "Caesar's". Jesus said to them, "Render to Caesar the things that are Caesar's, and to God the things that are God's." (R.S.V.)

Other typical instances are: Mark 2: 16–17 (Jesus and outcasts); 2: 23–27 (the treatment of the Sabbath); 3: 31–35 (Jesus' true relations); 9: 38–40 (the exorcist); 10: 13–15 (the reception of children); 10: 17–21 (the rich man); 12: 13–17 (the question of tribute); Luke 12: 13–15 (the question of the inheritance); 17: 20–21 (the coming of the Kingdom).

In these instances Jesus spoke on topics which were not only of interest to his immediate hearers but also of importance to the early Christians — the relation of Christianity to Judaism and Jewish institutions like the Sabbath and to the Roman rule, the right attitude towards 'outsiders' and children and rich people. When differences arose or there was discussion in the church about such matters, a story about Jesus which threw light upon the matter would be recalled and the narrative was remembered primarily for the sake of the saying to which it led up.

(ii) Miracle-stories. These tell of the power of Jesus in healing people and performing mighty works. Typical instances are Mark 1: 40–45 (the leper); 5: 1–20 (the madman of the Gerasene country); 5: 21-42 (Jairus' daughter); 9: 14-29 (the epileptic son); Luke 7: 11-17 (the widow's son). These stories generally follow much the same 'pattern'. There is given first a statement of the disease; then follows an appeal by the sufferer to Jesus. He makes his response — perhaps a question or a command; then comes the cure. Afterwards there is generally a comment — exclamations of wonder from the crowd or complaint from Jesus' opponents. Such stories would be of value not only in the Christian assemblies but also for missionary preaching. Heathen people, familiar with stories of miracles worked by the gods or their devotees, would be interested in these and would perhaps be able to appreciate the difference between these simply-told narratives and the marvellous and sometimes fantastic tales of pagan religions.

(iii) Biographical sketches of Jesus or of people who were associated with him. (Vincent Taylor calls these Stories about Jesus, while Dibelius' term is Tales.) Here there is more of a literary interest and it is not surprising to find many of them in Luke's Gospel. Accounts of the activities of Jesus include the visit to Nazareth (Mark 6: 1-6), a story about his childhood (Luke 2: 41-51), his baptism (Mark 1: 9-11) and temptations (Luke 4: 1-13; Matt. 4: 1-11), the incident at Caesarea Philippi (Mark 8: 27ff) and the transfiguration (Mark 9: 2ff).

Sketches of other people include the story of the sinful woman (Luke 7: 36-50), Mary and Martha (Luke 10: 38-42), Zacchaeus (Luke 19: 1-10) and the call of the first disciples (Mark 1: 16-20; cf. Luke 5: 1-11). In these cases there is given a fuller description of the circumstances than is found in the

Pronouncement-stories, and the emphasis is not so much on the saying of Jesus or on his healing power as on the characters of the people concerned. The early Christians would in this way have knowledge of the people in Jesus' own circle and his dealings with various types.

We must, however, beware of thinking that these three types of narrative form hard and fast categories (and we must certainly not imagine that the early Christians deliberately conceived these 'forms' and carefully arranged the oral material to fit into them!). The types sometimes overlap. It is, for instance, difficult to say definitely whether the story about Jesus' boyhood (Luke 2: 41-51) is best regarded as a Biography-story or a Pronouncement-story, since it concludes with a statement by Jesus himself. The narrative about Zacchaeus similarly might be put in either of these categories. The account of the cure of Bartimaeus (Mark 10: 46-52) might be classed as a Biography-story, since the man is named, or as a Miracle-story. The cure of the centurion's servant (Luke 7: 2-10; Matt. 8: 5-13) is a Miracle-story but it is also a Pronouncement-story, having its climax in a word of Jesus about the faith of a Gentile. We use the categories to help us to classify the material and to see more clearly the interests of the early Christians and their motives in preserving the oral traditions.

(iv) The teaching of Jesus, in sayings and parables. Just as the sayings of the Rabbis were remembered and treasured by their disciples, so the words of Jesus were repeated by the first apostles and passed on by word of mouth. Many of the statements of Jesus in the Gospels have no definite time or place associated with their utterance and they were probably repeated in the early church as detached utterances (e.g. Luke 12: 22ff; 17: 20–21). In some instances two writers do not agree about the place or time of an utterance of Jesus. Thus the saying about the world-wide nature of the Kingdom of God is attached in Matthew to the story of the centurion's servant (Matt. 8: 11–12), while Luke places it in another situation, on the way to Jerusalem (Luke 13: 28–29). The parables of the mustard seed and the leaven are placed in Matthew in the midst of a whole chapter devoted to parables (Matt. 13: 31–33) but they are isolated, in another situation, in Luke (13: 18–21). This supports the view that, like the stories, the sayings and parables of Jesus were told in the early Church in a somewhat fragmentary form; it would be left to the compiler of a written account later to set them out in order and to link them together. There must, however, have been many sayings which were not written down and so have been lost to us. One such statement, not recorded in our Gospels, would have perished if Paul had not quoted it or Luke recorded it in the Acts of the Apostles. In speaking to the leaders of the Ephesian church, Paul concluded his address with 'the words of the Lord Jesus, how he himself said, It is more blessed to give than to receive' (Acts 20: 35).

THE WRITING OF THE GOSPELS

All this material was thus in circulation in the early Church before the writing of the first of our Gospels. The episodes were told and retold as occasion demanded; the sayings and parables were recited. But we must not make too sharp a distinction between the oral and the writing period. We must not suppose that at a particular moment the disciples suddenly ceased to relate the stories and depended thenceforth simply on a written account. The two periods necessarily overlapped. Probably within twenty years of the crucifixion a collection of Jesus' sayings was made and written down. It is possible that some of the incidents also were written down, for use by preachers and teachers. This material was, however, still fragmentary in character. No attempt was made at a connected written account of Jesus' work from its beginning, after his baptism by John, to the end, culminating in the crucifixion and resurrection. And the oral material still continued to be told.

This material — mostly oral with probably some in writing — was the matter out of which the first of our written Gospels was made. The writer was not an author or biographer, in the modern sense. He was rather an editor or compiler, making use of the material already to a large extent familiar to his readers. In order to form a connected narrative, he had to link together the separate episodes and sayings. He introduced them with notes of time and place and supplied phrases to connect an incident with the preceding paragraph. Sometimes he added comments or gave a summary of Jesus' work and teaching (e.g. Mark 6: 53-56; cf. Matt. 4: 23-25). Explanatory notes were added, to help readers unfamiliar with the situation in Palestine (e.g. Mark 7: 3-4). Occasionally comments were added for the edification of the readers.

An illustration of this process of collecting and editing is provided by the accounts in Mark 2 and 3: 1-6. The writer (either Mark himself or a predecessor whose work he used at this point) gathered together a Miracle story — the paralysed man — (2: 1-12), the call of

Levi, a disciple (2: 14), a dispute over a meal with tax-collectors (2: 15-17), a discussion about fasting (2: 18-22), an incident on the Sabbath (2: 23-27) — a Pronouncement-story — and the cure of a man's withered hand on the Sabbath (3: 1-6). He thus produced a series of 'conflict-stories', in which the opposition to Jesus reaches a climax in a plot against him (3: 6). In Mark 9: 39-50 we have a collection of sayings which have little connection with each other, except that they are linked together by the repetition of certain 'key-words' and ideas. In Luke 16 a parable about a dishonest steward (vv. 1-8) is followed by a series of sayings about wealth and its responsibilities (vv. 9-13) which have no connection with the parable and very little relation with each other. In a similar way the writer of Matthew made a collection of parables about the Kingdom of God (13: 1-50), while Luke put together three parables about the lost in chapter 15.

There were a number of reasons why the oral period eventually came to an end and why the good news was committed to writing:

(a) The original disciples were going. James, the son of Zebedee, was the first of the twelve to be put to death (Acts 12: 2); this occurred about A.D. 42. By the second half of the first century it is possible that others had suffered a similar fate; in any case the apostles would be scattered in different parts of the world and were not immediately available with their first-hand reminiscences of the life of Jesus. The question inevitably arose: What was to happen when they were all gone? Would the oral story be lost or so changed by unauthorised additions that it could no longer be relied on?

(b) The first persecution of the Church by the

Romans accentuated this impulse to write. In A.D. 64, after the great fire of Rome, the emperor Nero tried to blame the Christians for it and attempted to stamp out the Church. It is probable that Peter and Paul were both put to death at this time. The Christians, deprived of their leaders and meeting together secretly, would want the story in a more permanent form than the oral traditions. Those who were suffering in this way would want to be assured of the historical origins of their faith, and others, drawn to the Church by the steadfastness of the Christians under persecution, would require something more than mere stories handed on by word of mouth.

(c) In A.D. 70 the Romans, after taking five years to crush the revolt of the Jews, took Jerusalem and destroyed the city and Temple. Before the final assault the Jewish Christians had fled across the Jordan to Pella. Jewish Christianity ceased practically to be of any importance in the Roman Empire, and the Church became almost an exclusively Gentile movement. This meant that Christianity was now cut off from its roots. The end of Jerusalem meant that the scene of the last days of Jesus' life was wiped out. The story must be preserved in a permanent and tangible form if it was not to become a tradition comparable to the legends of Greek and Roman 'sons of the gods', with no definite historical and geographical location.

(d) The needs of Christian worship were probably another factor. The early Church followed the form of worship in the synagogue, in having a reading from the Old Testament. Churches which had received letters from Paul, or possessed copies of those letters, probably supplemented the Old Testament reading by extracts from these. Possibly some of the teaching of

Jesus, already in written form, was also read at times. But there would be a demand, as time went on, for a fuller account of Jesus' ministry, which could be read consecutively, week after week.

So the telling of the stories gradually ceased and men came to rely on the written accounts. So now we turn to consider the Gospels as we have them in the New Testament.

CHAPTER II

THE BACKGROUND OF THE LIFE OF JESUS

IN ORDER to be able to appreciate and understand any great man of history, it is essential that we should know something of the people among whom he lived and from whom he came — not only their situation during his own time but also their history for a long period before his life. This is no less true of Jesus. Study of this constitutes the 'background' of the story in the Gospels.

I. *The historical background*

The simple statement that Jesus was a Jew and lived in Palestine supplies the key to much that is to be found in the Gospels. His people were the race known as the Hebrews, whose story is told in the Old Testament. This book constituted not only his Bible but also his text-book for history and literature.

The history of the Hebrews is a long one, which may be conveniently divided into these nine periods:

I. The Age of the patriarchs — from about 1800 B.C.
II. The Exodus from Egypt — about 1250 or 1400 B.C.
III. The settlement in Canaan.
IV. The monarchy — from about 1030 B.C.
V. The divided kingdom — about 930 to 722 B.C.

VI. The southern kingdom — from 722 to 586 B.C.
VII. The exile in Babylon — from 586 B.C.
VIII. The return from exile — from 538 B.C.
IX. Between the Old Testament and the New Testament.

More important than the facts of their history is the religion of the Hebrews. In the course of hundreds of years this progressed until the climax of their thought about God and man was reached in the time of the Exile in Babylon. Modern study of the Old Testament has thrown much light on this development and has enabled us to understand more fully many ideas and terms which occur in the New Testament.

Both their history and their religion constitute the historical background of the New Testament. The first disciples of Jesus were Jews, as were also the writers of the Gospels, with the exception of Luke. There are many references to the Old Testament books, some quite plain and some incidental. The height of the Old Testament religion is the belief in one God, who desires righteousness and love from his worshippers. This is called ethical monotheism and was the result of the teaching of the Hebrew prophets. This position was taken for granted by Jesus. He did not have to argue that there was one God or that he asked for a high standard of conduct from men. This was assumed by him and understood by his hearers. Jesus was able to use this as a foundation, to raise on it the structure of his own teaching.

II. *The political situation*

The overlords of Palestine in the first century were the Romans. In 63 B.C. Pompey had captured the country and entered Jerusalem. From that time Palestine was part of the Roman Empire, becoming incorporated in the province of Syria.

The Romans, however, often allowed native kings or chiefs to have power over their own territories. Herod the Great (whose family were originally not Jews) was permitted to call himself King of the Jews, from 37 B.C. As he worked with the Romans he was hated by the Jews. Partly to appeal to their religious loyalty and so conciliate them, he commenced, in 20 B.C., the building of the third Temple. On his death in 4 B.C. his kingdom was split up between three of his sons. Herod Archelaus was given Judea and Idumea, the southern portion. In A.D. 6 he was deposed by the Romans because of the complaints of the people and in his place a Roman procurator was appointed. The fifth procurator was Pontius Pilate, who ruled from A.D. 26 to 36.

Another son, Herod Philip, was given in 4 B.C. Iturea, north-east of the Jordan. He died in A.D. 34. Herod Antipas was given Galilee, in the north, and Perea, east of the Jordan valley. He is the Herod who is mentioned in the Gospels, in the time of Jesus. He married the daughter of the king of Damascus, but, attracted by Herodias, a niece of his who was the wife of his half-brother, he divorced his own wife and married her. In A.D. 39 he asked the Romans for the title of king (his official title was tetrarch, or ruler of a quarter of a province) but he was deposed by them and sent into exile.

In the time of Jesus the land of Palestine was thus divided into three portions: (*a*) Galilee and Perea, the territory of Herod Antipas; (*b*) Iturea and Trachonitis, ruled by Herod Philip; (*c*) Judea and Samaria, ruled

over by the Roman procurator. Samaria was inhabited by descendants of Assyrian colonists who had been imported into the territory of the northern kingdom of Israel when Samaria fell to the Assyrians in 722 B.C. They mingled with the people who remained, after the leading Israelites had been taken to Assyria. The Samaritans adopted the worship of Yahweh. On the return of the Jewish exiles to Judea from Babylon in 538 B.C., they offered to help in re-building the Temple (520 B.C.). Their help was refused by the Jews, so they tried to stop the building and fortification of the city of Jerusalem. Eventually they built their own rival Temple on Mount Gerizim. This was destroyed by a Jewish king in 110 B.C. All these events led to great bitterness between Jews and Samaritans, in which there was fault on both sides. In the time of Jesus, Jews who wished to go from Judea to Galilee would often cross to the eastern side of the Jordan, in order to avoid going through Samaria.

In A.D. 39 Herod Agrippa, grandson of Herod the Great, was made king of Judea (see Acts 12: 1-2 and 12: 20-23). On his death in A.D. 44 he was succeeded by his son, Herod Agrippa II (Acts 25: 13-27), who was the last of the Jewish kings. In A.D. 65 a revolt against the Romans broke out in Galilee. This spread and became a general rebellion. The Romans sent the general Vespasian to put it down and, when he returned to Rome in 69 to be Emperor, his son Titus carried on the war. In 70, after a terrible siege, he captured Jerusalem, destroyed the city and burnt the Temple. The Jewish nation was at an end, although the Jews persisted as a race and Judaism, of course, survived as a religion.

III. *The religious situation*

The Jews in the Roman Empire were allowed to keep their own religious beliefs and practices. The Roman power was generally tolerant in such matters, provided that the religious enthusiasm of subject people did not lead to public disturbance or attempts at revolt.

By the first century A.D. Judaism had become one of the chief legalistic religions of the world. This means that its observance consisted in certain religious duties or works. The man who performed these and carried out the Law was the pious man, blessed by God. The man who neglected them was considered outcast, from both human and divine society.

There were certain private or semi-private duties which strict Jews carried out. These included fasting — twice a week was the usual practice — almsgiving, which included paying of tithes to the priests and giving charity to beggars, and prayer — the making of prayers at set hours of the day, either in private or in the fellowship of others.

There was also public worship. The usual place was the synagogue, where services were held every Sabbath and during the week as well. The name 'synagogue' means simply a gathering or assembly and synagogue meetings were first held during the Exile in Babylon, when sacrificial worship was impossible, as the Temple at Jerusalem had been destroyed. Later, separate buildings were erected for the worship. By the first century synagogues were numerous, wherever Jews lived, in Palestine or elsewhere. The building was a square one, of simple design. There was no altar, but a platform, a reading-desk and a cupboard or curtained-off place at the end where the rolls of the Old Testament books were kept. The service also was simple — prayers, the chanting of Psalms, the reading of the Law and the Prophets, recitation of Hebrews passages and an address. The service was conducted by a Rabbi or one of the elders (or rulers) of the synagogue — prominent local men who managed the affairs of the synagogue.

Quite distinct from the synagogue was the Temple in Jerusalem. The first Temple was that of Solomon, which had been destroyed by the Babylonians when they took Jerusalem in 586 B.C. The second had been built after the return of the Jews from exile, in 520 B.C. The third was that of Herod the Great, which he commenced in 20 B.C. It was not finished in his own lifetime and was indeed not completed until A.D. 65, five years before it was completely destroyed by the Romans. The Temple building itself was entered only by the priests, and the innermost shrine, the Holy of Holies, was entered only by the High Priest and only on one day in the year — the Day of Atonement. Surrounding the building was a Court of the Priests, where there were altars on which the priests sacrificed. Outside this were two courts into which only Jews were allowed to go — the inner Court of the Men of Israel, where only Jewish men were permitted, and the Court of the Women, where any of the Jewish race might go. Still further outside, surrounding the whole area, was the great Court of the Gentiles, where anyone was allowed, and this had around it covered porticos.

The Temple was a place for sacrifice rather than for congregational worship such as was held in the synagogues. Animal sacrifices were performed every morning and evening by the priests. The Temple was

THE BACKGROUND OF THE LIFE OF JESUS

associated in particular with the great religious festivals such as Passover, Pentecost and Tabernacles. Jews from all over the world would then visit Jerusalem as pilgrims.

There were certain religious parties which laid stress on special aspects of their religion. These must not be thought of as parallel to modern 'denominations', for all worshipped in synagogues and sacrificed at the Temple. But there was frequently dispute between them.

Pharisees and Sadducees are often thought of together today but there were many differences between them. Both parties arose in the time of the Maccabees (from 160 B.C.) and represented different attitudes towards the Greek influence which was threatening Judaism.

The Pharisees believed fervently in the Old Testament but accepted also the 'oral traditions'. These were amplifications and interpretations of the written Law which had been made and handed down by scribes and Rabbis. The Pharisees thus believed in a future resurrection of the dead, after a stay in Hades, and, after that, a Day of Judgment by God. They trusted that God would himself set up his Kingdom; man's task was to observe the Law. They held to the hope of a Messiah, who would rule his Kingdom when he came.

No doubt many of the Pharisees were sincere worshippers of God and tried to please him. Such a one was Saul of Tarsus. But their insistence on keeping the Law and the traditions led them to be very stern towards all people who did not come up to their own standard. They tended to despise the common people. Many of the Pharisees were middle-class laymen —

business-men and shopkeepers. Their great interest was in the Law and the business of the synagogue. They disliked the rule of the Romans but were not prepared to help in a revolt against them. They held that when God was satisfied that the nation kept his Law fully, he would deliver them, in his own good time.

The Sadducees were more conservative in outlook. The origin of their name is obscure. It may have been taken from Zadok, a priest in the time of David and Solomon. They themselves derived it from a Hebrew word for 'the righteous'. It may, however, have been given to them because of their political activities.[1] The members of this party were mostly aristocrats and priests. They accepted the written Law of the Old Testament but rejected the oral traditions of the scribes. Consequently, as they did not believe in angels or demons, in a future resurrection or in a Messiah, they were frequently at variance with the Pharisees. They supported the rule of the Romans; indeed, they owed the security of their position to them.

The High Priest was a Sadducee and this party largely controlled the Sanhedrin. This was a Jewish Council of seventy-one members — frequently described in the Gospels as 'the chief priests and the scribes and the elders' — which had the right to try accusations of offence against the Jewish religious Law.

In the Gospels we find Pharisees opposing Jesus in Galilee. It was not until he came to Jerusalem that the Sadducees and priests began to take notice of his work. In the Acts the Sadducees are the first opponents of the disciples in Jerusalem.

The Zealots were an extreme religious and political party — fanatical nationalists. It is uncertain when

[1] See T. W. Manson: *The Servant-Messiah*, p. 16.

they actually arose, but a movement of this kind was started by Judas of Galilee, who revolted when the Romans attempted to take a census of Palestine in A.D. 6 (cf. Acts 5: 37). The Zealots were mainly responsible for the resistance to the Romans in the war of A.D. 65–70, which ended in the destruction of Jerusalem. They believed that God's kingdom could be set up on earth by force.

The Essenes are not mentioned in the New Testament; they represented the only attempt within Judaism at a monastic movement. They lived in communities, with their headquarters on the shores of the Dead Sea. Members (only men) were admitted after strict test and a period of probation. They were ascetics, wearing white garments, observing a strict discipline, keeping the Jewish laws of purity and indulging in ritual washing. It is generally thought that the community whose buildings have been unearthed at Qumran, west of the Dead Sea, the possessors of the scrolls found in the nearby caves, was an Essene settlement, although their fierce attitude towards the 'foreigners' (probably Romans) and their apocalyptic outlook would seem to link them with the Zealots.

The scribes were not a religious party but were a professional class. They were originally, as their name shows, the writers or copyists of the books of the Old Testament. From their acquaintance with these writings, they became the acknowledged teachers and interpreters of the Law. The majority of the scribes probably belonged to the Pharisee party but some were Sadducees.

Most of the ordinary people of Palestine did not ally themselves with any of these classes. They had not the leisure to study the Law minutely enough to be able to apply it diligently to every department of life; they were not Pharisees. They were not priests, so did not become Sadducees. They hated the Romans but were not prepared to rise in active revolt, so could not join with people like the Zealots. 'Sheep without a shepherd' well describes them. These were the people to whom the appeal of Jesus came with special force.

CHAPTER III

THE LIFE OF JESUS IN THE SYNOPTIC GOSPELS

FROM the second century onwards it has been customary to make a distinction between the first three Gospels and the fourth. Matthew, Mark and Luke give a similar outline of the work and ministry of Jesus and see it from much the same point of view. The fourth Gospel differs in chronology, in the presentation of the events narrated, in the style and matter of Jesus' teaching and in the place of most of his public work. Because of this the first three are classed together as the Synoptic Gospels (Greek: *sun*, together, and *opsis*, a view or sight). Many passages in these books can be put in parallel columns and thus 'seen together' in a synopsis.

The account of Jesus' work in the Synoptic Gospels falls into certain well-defined periods. A bare outline is given here, as a basis for the discussion in later chapters. For detailed notes on these passages the reader is referred to the author's *Life of Christ*.

I. *Jesus' birth and boyhood* (*Matt.* 1–2 ; *Luke* 1–2)

The two accounts agree in the statements that the birth of Jesus was announced beforehand, that he was born at Bethlehem, that Herod the Great was reigning (Matt. 2: 1; Luke 1: 5 implies this) and in the names of his parents. (As Herod died in the year we call 4 B.C.

it is evident that our dating of the years A.D. is 'out' by possibly half-a-dozen years.) In all other respects the accounts differ.

According to Luke 1: 26, Nazareth was the home of Joseph and Mary; they went to Bethlehem because of a Roman census. Luke tells of a visit from shepherds on the night of Jesus' birth, of presentation in the Temple and the words of Simeon and Anna. After this, Jesus' parents returned to Nazareth, 'their own city', and there remained. But in Matthew, Bethlehem was apparently the home of Joseph and Mary and Jesus was born in a house, not an inn. This Gospel tells of a visit of wise men from the east, of their interview with Herod, the search made for the child and the massacre of children of Bethlehem, when Jesus was about two years old. His parents fled with him to Egypt and after Herod's death they returned to Palestine and, instead of going back to Bethlehem, settled at Nazareth.

The two narratives are obviously at variance. Matthew's account seems to be dominated by a desire to find counterparts in the life of Jesus to statements in the Old Testament. Luke is generally more trustworthy as an historian and in his story of the journey from Nazareth to Bethlehem and the immediate return there of Joseph and Mary is more likely to be correct than Matthew's. There is no warrant for the popular idea that Joseph and Mary are responsible for the nativity stories, for they would both be dead long before either writer could get in touch with them. There is no independent historical evidence for the appearance of a star, the massacre at Bethlehem by Herod or a census in Palestine before the one instituted by the Romans in A.D. 6. The early Christians cherished these stories as emphasising the significance of the coming of Jesus.

II. *Jesus' work in Galilee* (*Mark* 1 *to* 7: 23; *Matt.* 3 *to* 15: 20; *Luke* 3 *to* 9: 17)

Jesus responded to the mission of John the Baptist; there came then to him the full (or the first) realisation of his vocation as Messiah and Servant (Mark 1: 11). In the temptation (Matt. 4: 1–11; Luke 4: 1–13) he was considering his methods of work and rejecting the current popular ideas of the Messiah. Except for one brief journey to the east of the lake (Mark 5: 1–20 and parallels), the bulk of Jesus' public work was then done in Galilee. There are four aspects of this:

(a) His deeds. These consist mainly of acts of healing. As a consequence, Jesus became popular with the crowds; he often told people who were cured not to say anything about it, apparently because he wanted to avoid such popularity. (See, e.g., Mark 1: 21 to 2: 12; 3: 1–6; 5: 1–43. Matt. 8: 5–13 (Luke 7: 2–10). Luke 7: 11–17.)

It is not possible to discuss here in full the question of Jesus' 'miracles'. The word is a vague and ambiguous one, meaning literally anything at which people tend to marvel. It is clear that what is a miracle to one age or nation might not be considered miraculous to people of another time or culture. The majority of Jesus' acts of healing are considered today as quite probable and it is notable that most of them were worked on people suffering from diseases which might be traced to mental or nervous disorders — paralysis, withered limbs, deafness and dumbness, blindness, leprosy (often a general name then for skin diseases of various kinds), epilepsy, attacks of insanity (attributed at that time to demon possession). There are two cases of the revivifying of people presumed dead — Jairus' daughter, who, according to Jesus, was not dead but asleep (Mark 5: 39), and the widow's son at Nain, who may have been in a coma, since it was forbidden to touch the bier of a dead person (Luke 7: 14). There are three so-called 'nature miracles' — the storm on the lake (Mark 4: 35-41), the walking on the water (Mark 6: 45-52) and the feeding of the people (Mark 6: 30-44; 8: 1-10 — variant accounts of the same incident). The fact that these are so few in number and seem to be considerably 'out of character' as activities of Jesus, as well as similar to the methods which he had rejected at the Temptation, has led some to conclude that what actually happened was not quite the same as the narratives we have in the Gospels. In each case a quite reasonable account of the situation can be given without the hypothesis that Jesus had control over the forces of nature or would use such power if he had it.

(b) His preaching and teaching. Mark sums this up as: 'The Kingdom of God is at hand' (1: 15). The nature of the kingdom is explained in parables (Mark 4: 1-32; Matt. 13: 1-52). There is also a section in Matt. 5-7 (the Sermon on the Mount) and Luke 6: 17-49, in which Jesus' teaching on various topics is collected together.

(c) The choice of twelve disciples. As was customary with eastern teachers, from the crowd which listened to him Jesus chose a small company (Mark. 3: 13-19). On these he could concentrate, in order to give them his teaching and to send them out on a preaching mission (Mark 6: 7-13; Matt. 10).

(d) Opposition. Jesus was opposed in his work and teaching by the religious authorities of the Jews (Mark 2–3; 7: 1–23). The reasons for this antagonism are discussed in a note appended to this chapter.

III. *Journeys to the north* (*Mark* 7: 24 *to* 9: 50; *Matt.* 15: 21 *to* 18: 35; *Luke* 9: 18–50)

While still in the north of Palestine, Jesus took two journeys outside Galilee. One was to Phoenicia, where he wished for quiet, but a Greek woman begged him to heal her daughter (Mark 7: 24–30). This is the only time that Jesus visited a 'foreign' country and one of the two occasions on which he had direct dealings with a Gentile; the other was a Roman centurion (Matt. 8: 5; Luke 7: 2). He also visited the territory of Herod Philip, around Caesarea Philippi (Mark 8: 27ff). The events there mark a turning point. In response to his questions, someone called Jesus Messiah for the first time. Peter at any rate, who may have spoken on behalf of the twelve, was able to conceive a different type of Messiah from the popular one. Jesus immediately began to talk about suffering and death as the lot of the Son of Man.

Thereafter his teaching was given mainly to the twelve. When he does speak to the crowd, it is to call would-be followers to sacrifice in his service (Mark 8: 34ff).

IV. *The journey to Jerusalem* (*Mark* 10; *Matt.* 19–20; *Luke* 9: 51 *to* 19: 28)

Matthew and Mark give a short account of a journey through Perea, east of the Jordan. Jesus received children who were brought to him, challenged a rich man to leave all and follow him and taught the ambitious disciples about true greatness.

Luke, however, says that Jesus went through Samaria. He records the churlish reception of his messengers by a Samaritan village (9: 51–56). He tells of various would-be followers (9: 57–62). He introduces in this section a large amount of teaching (10: 25–37; 11: 1 to 18: 14), some of it with parallels in Matthew but much of it distinctive, with a few incidents (10: 38–42; 17: 11–19).

The three Gospels come into line with the arrival at Jericho. There blind Bartimaeus was healed (Mark 10: 46–52). The significance of the incident is not only that this is the last miracle of Jesus, in Mark's narrative at least, but that the man called Jesus 'son of David'—the first time that Jesus had been acclaimed Messiah in public. Luke records also Jesus' meeting with Zacchaeus (19: 1–10).

V. *The last days in Jerusalem* (*Mark* 11–16; *Matt.* 21–28; *Luke* 19: 29 *to* 24: 53)

To enter the city, Jesus chose an ass, after making arrangement with a friend at Bethany for the animal to be ready (Mark 11: 1–11). It was the animal of peace, as used by ordinary people, in contrast to the horse, the animal of war and conquest. Jesus may also have had in mind Zechariah 9: 9—one of the few passages in the Old Testament where a king is spoken of as coming in peace and humbly. It is not agreed whether Jesus received a Messianic ovation from the people or not. Luke adds that he wept over the city, warning Jerusalem of the coming siege and destruction by the Romans (Luke 19: 41–44). Then he retired to Bethany.

The next day Jesus cleared the court of the Gentiles of those who made it into a market (Mark 11: 15–19).

Then a series of challenges was presented to him (Mark 11: 27 to 12: 34). The aim of his opponents was to get him to say something either against Jewish religious law or against the rule of Rome. So members of the Sanhedrin asked him whence he obtained his authority, Pharisees and Herodians pretended to consult him about the payment of taxes to Rome and Sadducees tried to trick him with a question about conditions in a resurrection. In each case Jesus refused to commit himself; he challenged his opponents to answer his counter-questions and laid down principles of abiding worth in each instance. Finally there came what appears to be a genuine enquiry by a scribe. The account ends on a brighter note, with Jesus commending a poor widow who gave sacrificially to the Temple treasury (Mark 12: 41–44).

On the Wednesday the priests plotted to kill Jesus, gaining unexpected help from Judas Iscariot (Mark 14: 1–2, 10–11). On Thursday Jesus made secret arrangements for the Passover meal with his disciples (Mark 14: 12–25; Luke 22: 7–27). There Jesus indicated that a traitor was among them. Acting as the host, he took the bread and wine and blessed them before the company ate and drank. He impressed on them that his body would be broken and his blood poured out. He referred to a 'covenant' which was now to be established. This was the term used in the Old Testament for the relationship between God and Israel. The covenant had been instituted by a sacrifice at Sinai (Exod. 24: 8). Jesus may also have been referring to the 'new covenant' which had been foreseen by Jeremiah (31: 31–34), in which God's law was written on the hearts of men.

After the meal Jesus warned his disciples that they

would forsake him, much to Peter's dismay. In Gethsemane Jesus was arrested by the Temple police, led by Judas to the place where they could seize him without interference. The disciples fled and Jesus was taken to trial (Mark 14: 26–52 and parallels). The first trial was a Jewish one, at which he was found guilty of blasphemy (Mark 14: 53–65). An official meeting of the Sanhedrin to confirm the sentence seems to be referred to in Mark 15: 1. It is uncertain whether the Sanhedrin had the right of capital punishment or not at this time; in any case it was safest to get the sentence of death confirmed by the Roman power.

The trial before Pontius Pilate is given briefly by Mark (15: 2–20), but Luke has a fuller account. He tells of a political accusation — that Jesus was a revolutionary, that he forbade payment of taxes and that he was 'Christ, a king' (or 'an anointed king'). Luke says that three times Pilate made an attempt to acquit Jesus and release him and also records an appearance before Herod Antipas (Luke 23: 1–25). The account of the crucifixion follows; by three o'clock in the afternoon of the Friday Jesus was dead (Mark 15: 21–41; Luke 23: 26–49). The final verdict was made by the Roman centurion in charge of the execution — 'This man was a son of God' (Mark 15: 39; cf. Luke 23: 47). He spoke, of course, as a pagan, who knew stories of the sons of the gods living amongst men, but for Mark's readers it would be a fitting climax to the account of 'the gospel of Jesus the Messiah, son of God' (Mark 1: 1).

Jesus' body was put in a tomb by Joseph of Arimathaea (Mark 15: 42–47), apparently as a temporary resting-place until the Sabbath was past. Some women visited the tomb early Sunday morning, where they were met by a young man who said that Jesus had risen and gone to Galilee. Mark's account breaks off abruptly at 16: 8 (see p. 79). Stories of appearances of Jesus are told in Matthew and Luke. The former says that the disciples went to Galilee, where Jesus met them and commissioned them to preach to the world (Matt. 28: 16–20). Luke says that they stayed in Jerusalem, at Jesus' express command. Two men walked with him to Emmaus, the eleven saw him in their midst and at Bethany he left them, after telling them to wait for the power which would equip them for their work (Luke 24: 13–53; cf. Acts 1: 1–9).

Thus the Gospels do not agree on the place where Jesus appeared to the disciples. Mark hints (14: 28; 16: 7) and Matthew states (28: 16) that they left Judea for Galilee, while Luke emphasises (24: 33, 49) that they remained near Jerusalem. Neither are they quite at one in their view of Jesus' nature. Matthew suggests an appearance which was not immediately recognisable or convincing, for he says that even some of the eleven 'doubted' (28: 17). Luke tends to think of a material body, for he says Jesus could be 'handled' and was able to eat (24: 39–43). In this he is at variance with the view of Paul (whose account of the resurrection appearances was written before our Gospels), who says nothing about an empty tomb and places the appearance to himself on the same level as those to the apostles and others, using the same Greek expression 'he was seen' (1 Cor. 15: 3–8).

There are two views about the activities of the disciples after Good Friday. Some think that they remained in the neighbourhood of Jerusalem, keeping together as one company, seeing Jesus at intervals until he eventually left them at what we call the 'ascension'. They continued in the city until the next Jewish festival,

Pentecost, seven weeks after Passover. Others consider that as soon as the Passover was ended the disciples returned to their own homes in Galilee and apparently resumed their normal occupations. There Jesus appeared to them and, when they were assured that he was alive and with them, they returned to Jerusalem to commence the work which he had commissioned them to do.

Note on the opposition to Jesus

A distinction must be made between the antagonism to Jesus in Galilee and the opposition in Jerusalem which eventually led to his death.

(a) *In Galilee.* His opponents here were scribes and Pharisees, who represented orthodox Judaism. There were four grounds for their attitude:

(i) They objected to the authority with which Jesus spoke and acted. The first reaction of the Capernaum congregation was one of astonishment at his teaching, 'for he taught as having authority and not as the scribes' (Mark 1: 22). The teaching of the scribes consisted mainly in discussion of detailed interpretation of particular passages in the Law and they often simply recounted the views of great Rabbis, setting one opinion against another. There was little that was original in their teaching. Jesus' authority was also one of deed. The people again remarked this when he had cured a demented man (Mark 1: 27) and after the healing of the paralytic: 'We never saw anything like this' (Mark 2: 12 R.S.V.). Matthew puts it: 'They glorified God, who had given such authority to men' (9: 8).

On one occasion at least Jesus met with a rebuff from the ordinary people. When he spoke in the synagogue at Nazareth, Mark says that the congregation were 'scandalised', for he was one of themselves and they knew his family (Mark 6: 2-3). He was unable to work amongst them. Luke says that he reminded them that the great prophets Elijah and Elisha had not confined their attention to Israelites but had helped foreigners as well (Luke 4: 24-29). This filled the people with anger and they turned Jesus out of the town.

The scribes could not deny Jesus' authority but they tried to account for it by saying that he was employed by the 'prince of demons' to do his cures. Beelzebub or Beelzebul in the Old Testament was the name of a Philistine god and was used in Jesus' day to denote the power which was over the kingdom of evil. Jesus first pointed out the absurdity of such an accusation; to say that he used Beelzebub to drive out demons would mean civil war. Surely a stronger than Beelzebub had bound him and was 'spoiling his house' or dominion (Mark 3: 23-27). In the parallel in Matthew and Luke Jesus says that the only way to account for his authority was to see that he was using the power of God and hence the reign of God had come among men (Matt. 12: 28-30; Luke 11: 20-22).

(ii) Jesus ignored the distinction between loyal and law-abiding men and 'sinners'. This term, when used in the Gospels, generally denotes people who did not observe strictly the Jewish religious regulations and commandments, such as the keeping of the Sabbath or the prohibitions about food or mixing with foreigners. His opponents argued that if he were a true religious teacher he would observe the laws and have nothing to do with such 'outcasts'.

It was complained that Jesus was 'a friend of tax-collectors and sinners' (Luke 7: 34; cf. Luke 15: 1-2).

The publicans (this English term comes from the Latin *publicanus* — a man engaged on business for the State) collected taxes from the Jews on behalf of the Romans. This in itself was sufficient to call forth dislike and hatred from all patriotic Jews. The publicans further gathered more than the 'legal' amount of taxation; it was the only way in which they could make a living out of their occupation. They also had to mix with Gentiles in the course of their business and did not observe the strict religious regulations. They were 'outsiders'. Jesus, however, called Levi from his office to be a disciple (Mark 2: 14) and later sat down at a meal with many such men, who followed him. Jesus, in reply to a complaint by scribes of the Pharisee party, referred to the practice of a doctor. He had come with the purpose of inviting 'sinners', not righteous people (Mark 2: 17). Later on, in Jericho, he invited himself to the house of the rich tax-collector Zacchaeus, again calling forth complaint from the bystanders (Luke 19: 7).

(iii) Jesus was also opposed because he and his disciples did not strictly observe the Law. It has been calculated that in the Old Testament there are 613 commands — 365 positive ones and 248 negative ones. These related to practically every department of personal and social life and to these were added the 'oral traditions', amplifications of the written Law to make it apply to current conditions. If a man did not observe these, or if he flagrantly disregarded one of the regulations generally observed by strict Jews, he was an irreligious man.

The Pharisees complained that Jesus' disciples ate their food with 'defiled' or 'unwashed' hands (Mark 7: 2). This was not a matter of hygiene but of ritual.

The word means literally secular or profane, as opposed to holy or consecrated. Strict Jews took care to wash their hands diligently and ceremonially, since they might have had contact in the market with Gentiles or other people outside the Jewish Law. In reply, Jesus attacked the whole observance of the 'traditions of the elders'. A man might swear that his property was 'corban' — dedicated — and according to the Law he must keep his oath at all costs and not touch the money, even if it meant his parents went in need (7: 8–13). Then Jesus developed his own view about impurity, declaring that it was not what a man ate which made him clean or unclean but the nature of his thoughts and impulses.

On another occasion, in a Pharisee's house, complaint was made that Jesus himself had not washed before the meal (Luke 11: 38). Here Jesus pointed out that the Pharisees attended to external cleanliness but ignored the requirements of inward purity (11: 39–41; the phrase 'give alms' in verse 41 is probably a Greek mistranslation of an Aramaic word for 'cleanse' as in Matt. 23: 26).

The Pharisees complained that Jesus' disciples did not observe the Jewish fasts. Again Jesus defended them, pointing out that his company was more of a marriage-party than a mourning-party (Mark 2: 18–19). Jesus shows the impossibility of combining old and new. The conventional religion of Judaism could not be patched up to make Jesus' teaching fit it; it was impossible to contain his new wine in the old receptacles (2: 21–22).

Jesus' attitude to the Jewish observances is exemplified in the stories which tell of conflict about the Sabbath. The Pharisees held that no work must be done at all on the Sabbath, or anything which could be considered the equivalent of work. To pluck the ears of corn at harvest time and rub them in the hands was counted by the Rabbis to be the same as reaping and threshing — work which was obviously forbidden on the Sabbath. It was complained that Jesus' disciples did this as they walked through the fields (Mark 2: 23-24). He first pointed out that even the Law must be subservient to human needs, giving a case from Hebrew history about David. He concluded with the statement that the Sabbath was made for the benefit of man; man was not made in order to be concerned about keeping the Sabbath (verse 27).

The Jewish Law forbade even a doctor to do his work on the Sabbath, unless it was a case of life or death. Jesus cured a man with a withered hand — possibly deliberately placed by the door of the synagogue, so that Jesus' enemies might find fault with him, whatever he did. Jesus pointed out that to neglect the chance of healing the man and so doing good would be equivalent to condemning him to further suffering (Mark 3: 4). This applied whether the day was a Sabbath or not. His opponents could not answer his argument so he proceeded to heal the man.

Luke has two other stories of healing on the Sabbath. The infirm woman was perhaps a sufferer from some form of nervous prostration. Jesus replied to his critics that the Law allowed acts of kindness on the Sabbath even to animals; how much more should this apply to human beings (Luke 13: 10-16). Jesus was again dining with a Pharisee when a man with dropsy entered. Jesus asked a question like that in Mark 3: 4 and added that, whether the Law allowed it or not, a Jew would rescue a stricken animal on the Sabbath;

how much more must a man be rescued (Luke 14: 1–5).

In all these cases Jesus did not say that the Sabbath should not be kept. What he was against was the narrow spirit which laid down specific regulations and condemned those who did not or could not rigidly observe them; this made the Sabbath a burden rather than a delight and resulted in the denial of the spirit of human kindness, thus defeating the end for which the Sabbath was inaugurated — the refreshment of a man's spirit in fellowship with God.

(iv) Jesus counter-attacked to the accusations of his enemies. When they accused him of using the power of Beelzebub, he declared that they were ascribing to the agency of an evil power that which was obviously the work of the Spirit of God. This failure to differentiate between good and evil was 'blasphemy against the Spirit' of holiness. It rendered a man incapable of moral discrimination. It was sin in its fulness or an 'eternal sin' which could not be forgiven, for such a man was incapable of receiving forgiveness (Mark 3: 28–29). We have seen him also counter-attacking in his remarks about 'corban' and the Jewish attitude towards the Sabbath, which meant in effect that they were doing evil on the holy day (Mark 3: 4).

Jesus warned his hearers in Jerusalem about the scribes, for their show and deceit (Mark 12: 38–40). Earlier he castigated the Pharisees and the lawyers (much the same as the scribes) for imposing their rules upon people and not living up to their own principles (Luke 11: 42–52). Matthew compiled a long discourse by combining these two passages, with additional matter from his own sources (23: 1–36). The condemnation of the Pharisees and their associates is here sometimes very bitter and it is probable that the writer has exaggerated the faults of the Pharisees and the vehemence of Jesus' denunciation. Even when we make allowance for this, however, we can see that Jesus had some forceful things to say about the principles and practices of the Jewish religious leaders. His words would not improve the strained relations between them and him.

(b) *In Jerusalem*. Here the Pharisees fall into the background. They are mentioned only once in Mark, when they united with the Herodians (12: 13; cf. 3: 6). In Jerusalem Jesus' enemies were the priests and members of the Sanhedrin; most of these would be adherents of the Sadducee party. The reasons for the opposition are quite different from those which we saw in Galilee.

It was probably Jesus' action in clearing the Court of the Gentiles of those who were buying and selling and changing money which brought him to the notice of the priests. Traders sold materials for sacrifices there and Jews who came from foreign countries were supplied with the special Temple money with which they were required to pay a tax. All this trading, which led to fleecing of the pilgrims, was done with the full consent of the authorities. The priests are mentioned for the first time when a deputation from the Sanhedrin came to demand his authority 'for doing these things' (Mark 11: 27-28). The Sadducees are named as bringing a question about the resurrection with the intention of trapping Jesus (Mark 12: 18ff). By contrast to these priestly authorities, a scribe was praised and declared to be 'not far from the Kingdom of God' (12: 34).

'The chief priests and the scribes' were those who sought to arrest Jesus and kill him (Mark 14: 1-2) and it was to the chief priests that Judas went with his offer of betrayal (14: 10). Jesus was arrested by 'a multitude with swords and staves' from the Sanhedrin — probably members of the priestly police force which kept order in the Temple Courts (14: 43). It was by the high priest and other members of the Sanhedrin that Jesus was tried first of all (14: 53; 15: 1) and it was they who brought him before Pilate and stirred up the people to demand the release of Barabbas (15: 11; cf. Luke 23: 13). When he was on the cross, the chief priests, with the scribes, mocked him as being unable to save himself (Mark 15: 31).

The grounds of the antagonism in Jerusalem appear in the accusations made against Jesus at the trial before the Sanhedrin. Nothing is said about his disregard of Sabbath regulations, of his attitude towards the legal traditions, of his mixing with outcasts. Instead, he was accused of having said that he would destroy the Temple and build another one, an immaterial Temple, in three days. The truth behind this statement was probably that Jesus foresaw the end of the Temple. Mark 13: 2 says he definitely spoke of this. Jesus could perceive the consequences of the attitude of the Jews towards the Romans — that it would mean the end of them as a nation, the destruction of Jerusalem. This is the point of the statements in Luke 13: 3, 5 — that unless the Jews repented (changed their minds and ways), they would all perish like the rebellious Galileans or the men who were killed while undermining a Roman fortification.

His enemies, hearing reports of such words, twisted them into a false accusation (Mark 14: 57 — he stresses that it was false witness) that he said he would destroy the Temple. This would mean an attack on Judaism at its heart — the sacrificial system. There may be also a hint here that his enemies, in making this accusation, may have realised what his own disciples did not — that his teaching and spirit were incompatible with the continuance of the sacrificial system at Jerusalem. To 'build another made without hands' in three days (an eastern expression for a very short time) probably meant that the requirements of true worship could be satisfied without a material Temple; perhaps Jesus was thinking of the invisible Kingdom of God. Unable, however, to get Jesus guilty on this charge, the high priest dramatically challenged him to say whether he was the Messiah or not. On his answering, he was condemned for blasphemy against God. The penalty for this was death by stoning (Lev. 24: 16).

The grounds on which Jesus was finally condemned and executed had nothing to do with the charges made against him in Galilee and little in common with the reasons for the antagonism of the members of the Sanhedrin. The three charges which the priests made before Pilate (Luke 23: 2) were intended to mean that the man was politically dangerous to the Roman state (see p. 32). Historically, Jesus was crucified as a criminal who had committed an offence against Rome. Although there was a tendency to blame the Jews, Pilate had the final word and it was the Roman power which had him executed. The *titulus* which, as customary in such executions, was put over the head of the crucified man, read 'The king of the Jews' (Mark 15: 26). For any man to claim to be king without the sanction of Rome was a crime punishable by death. Luke records the dramatic and ironical fact that the only man who recognised Jesus as having a kingdom was a guilty and condemned criminal (Luke 23: 42).

CHAPTER IV

THE FIRST WRITTEN GOSPEL

The Synoptic Problem

A problem exists whenever there are facts which have to be accounted for. This is true in all studies — science, history, literature. The synoptic problem arises from the facts about the contents of the three Gospels — facts which are plain to any careful reader. Three questions demand to be answered: Why are the three books so much alike? At the same time, why do they differ in some ways? What is the solution of the problem which most fully accounts of these facts?

(i) The similarities in the three Gospels. All three have the same general outline of the life of Jesus. This outline has been described in the previous chapter — his work in Galilee, visits to the north, a journey to Jerusalem, the last days there. One would expect the writer of a Gospel to include much of this matter and for the three books to overlap to some extent; but all three include it in the same order. Events frequently follow one another in the same sequence. When one account diverges, the three always return to the common order.[1]

Further, when we study these parallel passages, whether of incident or of teaching, we find a remarkable

---

[1] This can be clearly seen by a study of A. Barr's *Diagram of Synoptic Relations*.

verbal similarity; sometimes the wording is almost identical for whole sentences.[1] The following passages are typical and it is worth while studying them in detail:

The healing of the paralytic (Matt. 9: 1–8; Mark 2: 1–12; Luke 5: 17–26).

The question of fasting (Matt. 9: 14–17; Mark 2: 18–22; Luke 5: 33–39).

The parable of the mustard seed (Matt. 13: 31–32; Mark 4: 30–32; Luke 13: 18–19).

The feeding of the five thousand (Matt. 14: 13–21; Mark 6: 30–44; Luke 9: 10–17).

The rich man (Matt. 19: 16–22; Mark 10: 17–22; Luke 18: 18–23).

The healing of Bartimaeus (Matt. 20: 29–34; Mark 10: 46–52; Luke 18: 35–43).

The challenge to Jesus' authority (Matt. 21: 23–27; Mark 11: 27–33; Luke 20: 1–8).

The question of tribute (Matt. 22: 15–22; Mark 12: 13–17; Luke 20: 20–26).

Peter's denials (Matt. 26: 69–75; Mark 14: 66–72; Luke 22: 56–62).

In other cases the parallel matter is found in only two Gospels. Occasionally this is in Mark and either Matthew or Luke but most frequently it is in Matthew and Luke only. The following are typical passages:

The calling of disciples (Matt. 4: 18–22; Mark 1: 16–20).

[1] A 'synopsis' of the Gospels, in which the accounts are set forth in adjacent columns, is invaluable here — e.g. A. Huck: *Gospel Parallels* (in English). The Greek text is given in Huck's *Synopsis of the First Three Gospels*.

Jesus and scribal tradition (Matt. 15: 1–20; Mark 7: 1–23).

The sons of Zebedee (Matt. 20: 20–28; Mark 10: 35–45).

The anointing at Bethany (Matt. 26: 6–13; Mark 14: 3–9).

The widows' mites (Mark 12: 41–44; Luke 21: 1–4).

John the Baptist's preaching (Matt. 3: 7–10; Luke 3: 7–9).

Teaching on judging others (Matt. 7: 1–6; Luke 6: 37–38, 41–42).

Teaching on anxiety (Matt. 6: 25–33; Luke 12: 22–31).

The healing of a centurion's servant (Matt. 8: 5–13; Luke 7:1–10).

John's question from prison (Matt. 11: 2–19; Luke 7: 18–35).

The parable of the leaven (Matt. 13: 33; Luke 13: 20–21).

Jesus' lament over Jerusalem (Matt. 23: 37–39; Luke 13: 34–35).

Anyone who studies these parallel passages carefully must be convinced that a problem exists and that there must be some connection between the three Gospels.

(ii) The differences between the three Gospels. The Synoptics are not entirely alike. If they were, there would be no real problem; they would obviously be copies of each other or of an earlier work. There are again two ways in which the differences appear — in the order of events and in the wording in parallel passages.

There are variations within the same general Synoptic scheme of events. The cures of the demoniac, the woman and Jairus' daughter are all told in this order in the three Gospels, but in Mark and Luke they come after Jesus' teaching in parables, but before it in Matthew. The account of the rejection of Jesus at Nazareth comes at much the same point in Matthew (13: 53–58) and in Mark (6: 1–6), but is considerably earlier in Luke (4: 16–30). Teaching which is given in Mark (13: 9–13) in Jerusalem in the last week is said in Matthew (10: 17–22) to have been delivered in Galilee, early in the ministry.

In parallel passages the wording is generally not exactly the same. Study of the passages enumerated above will have amply demonstrated this. Sometimes it seems as if one Gospel and sometimes another has the more vivid phrase or graphic description or has reproduced more faithfully the note of Jesus' teaching.

A further difference is that each of the Gospels has matter which is not found elsewhere. This is very small in the case of Mark — only about thirty verses, consisting of one parable, two healing acts and a few particulars here and there in the narrative. Matthew has a considerable amount of Jesus' teaching which is not in Mark or Luke and some additional particulars in common narratives. Luke has a large amount of matter peculiar to this book consisting of both incidents and parables and sayings. Both Matthew and Luke record stories about the birth and infancy of Jesus, but the accounts are quite different. At the end of each of these two Gospels there are recorded appearances of Jesus after the resurrection, but again they differ and even conflict in some particulars.

Just as the similarities show that there must be some connection between the three Gospels, so the differences show that they must have been written independently. Each writer tells the story from his own point of view.

THE FIRST WRITTEN GOSPEL

The opening words of each Gospel well illustrate this. Matthew starts with a genealogy of Jesus, like a typical Jewish book, similar to some of the Old Testament books. Mark has a 'heading', which sounds like a proclamation, and then, after a passing reference to the Old Testament, plunges into the story of John the Baptist — blunt and straightforward, like the remainder of the book. Luke commences with a carefully worded introduction and dedication to Theophilus, and his is indeed the most literary of all the Gospels.

These facts constitute the Synoptic Problem. However 'uncritical' a reader may claim to be, he cannot fail to be struck by these facts and if he desires to understand the Gospels fully he is bound to proceed to the questions: What is the relation between the three books? Why are they so much alike and yet so different? What can we deduce from this study about the writers and about the methods which they used in composing their books?

SOLUTIONS OF THE SYNOPTIC PROBLEM

To these questions various answers have been given:

(i) One traditional answer has been that God inspired the evangelists to write and so they must agree when they record the teaching and acts of Jesus. There are two main difficulties in this view. One is that it conceives God as dictating to men what they were to put down, without allowing for their natural human inclination and ability. This is at variance with all that we know of the ways of God with men and with all that the Bible teaches about inspiration. The second objection is that the theory does not fit the facts. While it might be held to account for the similarities and verbal parallels, it does not account for the differences. Why should God inspire one man to say that James and John came to Jesus with a request (Mark 10: 35) but tell another man to write that their mother came? (Matt. 20: 20). Why should he dictate, 'How canst thou say . . .?' to one writer (Luke 6: 42), but 'How wilt thou say . . .?' to another? (Matt. 7: 4). Why should he instruct Mark to write a full and vivid account of many a healing act of Jesus (e.g. 5: 1–20 and 9: 14–29) but inspire Matthew to write a shorter and considerably less vivid account? (8: 28–34 and 17: 14–20). Why, if both writers were verbally inspired by God, should Matthew's Gospel say that the Roman centurion came himself to Jesus with a request that he would heal his Servant (8: 5ff), while in Luke's account the centurion never appears at all but sends his message through others (7: 3ff)?

If it is replied that God must work through the interests of each individual and leave an author to write in his own style and use his own intelligence and critical capacity, this surrenders the whole case for 'verbal inspiration'. This is the very problem with which we are concerned — why three accounts should differ, as well as why they agree — and it is no real answer to say simply that they were 'inspired' to do so. This theory indeed does not arise from a study of the books themselves and the problem which they present but from a preconceived notion of 'inspiration' which will not bear examination when confronted with the facts.

(ii) Another traditional explanation is the 'oral hypothesis'. Each writer is held to be dependent on the oral tradition, such as we have discussed in chapter I. They wrote independently but happened to use similar words and phrases and kept to the same general order because they faithfully adhered to the oral accounts.

The first difficulty here is that this theory regards the oral traditions as having assumed a fixed form not only in the relation of particular incidents or sections of teaching but also in the general order of the narrative. There is no gound for this assumption and it is very unlikely in itself; the traditions circulated in the Church as separate episodes, not as one connected historical narrative, and we can still discern the fragmentary nature of the stories even in our written Gospels. It is also very improbable that the oral traditions would have attained such fixity of form and wording and that three writers, rendering the tradition independently and probably in different parts of the Roman world, would agree in their phraseology and order of events in the way that the three Synoptists do.

This theory further does not explain the variations either in wording or in order. In some instances the verbal differences are due to stylistic and grammatical alterations. This suggests not oral traditions only but a written document which is being used. How also are we to account, on this view, for the matter found in Matthew and Luke but not in Mark — again often similar in wording but with subtle and characteristic alterations — or the matter which is peculiar to Matthew or to Luke? If this was part of the 'standard' oral tradition, why was it omitted by the other writers?

We are therefore forced to the conclusion that something more than simply oral tradition lies behind the three accounts and that there is a literary connection between them. A documentary hypothesis must be examined. The possibilities here are many — that all three used the same document or more than one document or that one Gospel was written first and the other two made use of it — if so, which one?

(iii) The first documentary theory was that Matthew was written first and that Mark abbreviated this book. Augustine (about A.D. 400) suggested this; he regarded Mark as the 'attendant and abbreviator of Matthew' (*pedisequus et breviator Matthaei*). This view was put forward because Mark's Gospel is shorter than Matthew's and much of the Matthaean matter is not found in Mark.

There are two main objections here. The first impression of Mark, as being shorter than Matthew, is deceptive, for in parallel narratives Mark is almost always the longer account. The following narratives as told in the two books occupy the number of verses indicated:

The healing of the paralytic: Mark 12, Matthew 7 verses.

The Gerasene madman: Mark 20, Matthew 7 verses.

Jairus' daughter and the healing of a woman: Mark 23, Matthew 9 verses.

The feeding of the five thousand: Mark 15, Matthew 9 verses.

The healing of the epileptic son: Mark 16, Matthew 7 verses.

In these and other instances Mark's narrative is much more vivid and lifelike than Matthew's, which is often tame in comparison and omits vital points. No 'abbreviator' of Matthew would take these narratives and make them into Mark's fuller accounts. The reverse is much more likely.

The other objection is that so much valuable matter found in Matthew is missing in Mark. Why should an 'abbreviator' or editor omit the Sermon on the Mount and parables such as the treasure and the pearl merchant, the labourers in the vineyard, the ten virgins, the sheep and the goats? Why should he ignore the story of Jesus' birth and infancy and commence his account with John the Baptist's work, in the abrupt way that Mark does?

(iv) A documentary theory popular in some circles in the last century was the view that there was a primitive written gospel which was used by all three writers. (German critics called this *Urevangelium*). This might account for the places where the three agree in order of events or in wording. But it does not take into account the matter which is common to Luke and Matthew, but not found in Mark. If this was in the primitive Gospel, why did Mark omit it? Neither can it account for the matter peculiar to Matthew or to Luke. One must assume here also, as with the hypothesis of the priority of Matthew, that the writer of Mark deliberately omitted much that was valuable of the teaching and activitives of Jesus and yet managed to produce a book which gives a straightforward impression of a simple and vivid narrative.

It is thus difficult to assign a limit to this supposed primitive Gospel. If we limit its contents to the parallels in all three Gospels, we are making it practically identical with our Mark; this is quite a feasible suggestion, but in the process the primitive document, as a separate identity, has disappeared! There is also the great difficulty that no trace of such a document can be found and there is no support in early Church writings for its existence.

This view, like that of Augustine, has now generally been abandoned. It has become clear, from study of the parallel passages and the similarity in the order of the narrative, that the literary connection is between the three Gospels as we have them — that one account was written first and that the other two writers made use of it. The suggestion was made by C. Lachmann in 1835 that Mark was the first to be written and was used by the authors of Matthew and Luke. This theory was developed and soon accepted by leading scholars. It has been thoroughly tested by minute study of the Gospels in the original Greek and is the solution accepted by the vast majority of New Testament scholars today.

REASONS FOR BELIEVING IN THE PRIORITY OF MARK

(i) Almost the whole of Mark's Gospel is found in Matthew or Luke or both. Ninety-five per cent of its total matter is contained in Matthew, while about sixty-five per cent of it is in Luke. In Mark there are 662 verses; of these, 609 have parallels in Matthew and 357 in Luke (with an additional 95 which are doubtful, as the Lukan parallel is not so exact). There are only thirty verses in Mark which have no parallel elsewhere.

(ii) The correspondence of language is striking. More than half the Greek words used in Mark are reproduced in parallel sections in the other two Gospels; in particular passages the percentage is often higher. Where Matthew or Luke diverge, Mark is generally common to one of them; there are very few cases in which Matthew and Luke agree in their language, as against Mark. The passages enumerated on p. 44 are all illustrations of this. One passage is given here in full, so that the correspondence and divergence of language can be studied. Comment on this and other parallel sections is given below, under (vi):

MATTHEW 21: 23-27.	MARK 11: 27-33.	LUKE 20: 1-8.
23 And when he was come into the temple, the chief priests and the elders of the people came unto him as he was teaching, and said, By what authority doest thou these things? and who gave thee this authority? 24 And Jesus answered and said unto them, I also will ask you one question, which if ye tell me, I likewise will tell you by what authority I do these things. 25 The baptism of John, whence was it? from heaven or from men? And they reasoned with themselves, saying, If we shall say, From heaven; he will say unto us, Why then 26 did ye not believe him? But if we shall say, From men; we fear the multitude; for all hold John as a 27 prophet. And they answered Jesus, and said, We know not, He also said unto them, Neither tell I you by what authority I do these things.	27 And they come again to Jerusalem: and as he was walking in the temple, there come to him the chief priests, and the scribes, and 28 the elders; and they said unto him, By what authority doest thou these things? or who gave thee this authority to do these 29 things? And Jesus said unto them, I will ask of you one question, and answer me, and I will tell you by what authority I do 30 these things. The baptism of John, was it from heaven, or from men? answer me. 31 And they reasoned with themselves, saying, If we shall say, From heaven; he will say, Why then did ye 32 not believe him? But should we say, From men — they feared the people: for all verily held John to be a 33 prophet. And they answered Jesus and say, We know not. And Jesus saith unto them, Neither tell I you by what authority I do these things.	1 And it came to pass, on one of the days, as he was teaching the people in the temple, and preaching the gospel, there came upon him the chief priests and the scribes with 2 the elders; and they spake, saying unto him, Tell us: By what authority doest thou these things? or who is he that gave thee this authority? And he answered and said 3 unto them, I also will ask you a question; and tell me: the bap-4 tism of John, was it from heaven, or from men? And they rea-5 soned with themselves, saying, From heaven; he will say, Why then we shall 6 believe him? But if we shall say, From men; all the people will stone us: for they be persuaded that John was a prophet. 7 And they answered, that they knew not whence it was. And 8 Jesus said unto them, Neither tell I you by what authority I do these things.

(iii) The common order of events throughout is that of Mark. The general Synoptic outline of Jesus' life has been given in chapter III. Sometimes Matthew and sometimes Luke departs from the Markan order, but they never do so at the same point and they always return to it. The first fourteen chapters of Matthew correspond to the first six of Mark. (Matthew's total is more because the writer has included matter from other sources.) Matthew diverges from the Markan order in putting earlier the appointment of the twelve disciples (Mark 3: 13ff; Matt. 10: 1ff), in order to introduce instruction given especially to them. The story of the 'legion' madman (Mark 5: 1-20) is put before the healing of the paralytic (Mark 2: 1-12; Matt. 8: 28ff), and the story of Jairus' daughter and the woman (Mark 5: 21-43) is inserted into the middle of the conflict stories (Matt. 9: 18-26) which are found in Mark 2. (In each case, it may be noted, the Markan order is far more likely to be the original.) The writer of Matthew, after these divergences, always returns to Mark's order. From chapter 14 onwards the order in Matthew is Mark's without any divergence in sequence of events.

Where Luke has matter parallel with Mark, in no important place does he diverge from Mark's sequence. He gives blocks of Markan matter alternating with blocks of non-Markan matter, and the Markan blocks are in the same order as they are found in Mark's Gospel. Thus there is here a phenomenon similar to that observed in the matter of language. Whenever the other two writers depart from Mark, they never do so at the same point; and they always return to it, as if Mark were the common basis for their narratives.

(iv) Mark is the shortest of the three Gospels. It is far more likely that the other two made use of this brief book and expanded it with other material which was at hand, than that the writer of Mark attempted a 'cut' version of either of the others.

(v) Mark's Gospel is a *relatively* simple document, when compared with the others. (This must not be taken to mean that Mark is a 'simple human biography' of Jesus.) In Mark, Jesus is portrayed as the Messiah

THE FIRST WRITTEN GOSPEL

and Son of Man, and emphasis is laid upon his deeds and acts of power. There is little systematic teaching — a few parables in 4: 1–32, sayings in 9: 39–50 and an apocalyptic discourse in chapter 13. The other two Gospels show further developments from this 'basic' portrait of Jesus and his work, Matthew seeking to emphasise the Judaistic nature of Jesus' teaching and work and Luke portraying Jesus' universal message. Each writer thus, in an opposite direction, completes the portrait which Mark, in his central position, has outlined.

(vi) When the parallel passages are studied in detail and the divergences in language are examined, we can see reasons why Matthew or Luke should have altered Mark but no reason why the reverse process should have taken place. This is seen especially in four ways:

(a) Mark's Greek style is rough-and-ready, sometimes with grammatical slips and peculiar constructions. He is fond of the present tense in narrating (in 151 instances) but he does not always keep to it in the course of a paragraph. Matthew uses this twenty-one times and Luke only once, in such passages. In the narrative reproduced on p. 53 Mark varies his tenses from the present to the past, while Matthew and Luke both keep to the past throughout. Mark repeats, for emphasis, phrases like 'to do these things' (11: 28) and 'Answer me' (11: 29, 30); the other two omit these as unnecessary; perhaps they thought the last one too brusque. Mark has an unfinished sentence which dramatically breaks off with the thoughts of Jesus' opponents, who were muttering to themselves: 'But if we shall say, From men — they feared the people . . .' The other two writers smooth it out: 'If we shall say, From men, we fear the multitude

(Matt. 21: 26); if we shall say from men, all the people will stone us' (Luke 20: 6). Mark tends to repeat himself. He says that tax-collectors and sinners sat down with Jesus and his disciples, and adds: 'for there were many and they followed him' (Mark 2: 15). Both Matthew and Luke omit this as unnecessary. Mark says: 'at even, when the sun set' (1: 32); Matthew reproduces 'when even was come' (8: 16); and Luke 'when the sun was setting' (4: 40).

(b) Particular words in Mark are changed in Matthew or Luke, to make them more intelligible or acceptable to their readers. Mark sometimes gives the actual Aramaic words used by Jesus and his contemporaries in Palestine — Talitha Cumi (5: 41), Ephphatha (7: 34), Corban (7: 11), Rabboni (10: 51), Golgotha (15: 34). Luke keeps none of the Aramaic words but substitutes Greek ones generally, while Matthew keeps only Golgotha. Mark uses a 'popular' word when he describes the pallet on which the paralytic lay (Greek *krabattos* — a poor man's mat) (Mark 2: 4, 11–12). The other two writers did not like to employ this and Matthew substituted the ordinary Greek word for 'bed' (9: 2, 6), although it would be impossible to pick up this and walk home with it. Luke likewise first describes it as a 'bed' (5: 18), then he changes it to 'couch' (5: 19, 24) and then, realising the unsuitability of these words, falls back on 'the thing he was lying on'! (5: 25). Mark, in describing Peter after his denial of Jesus, uses a colloquial expression which should probably be translated: 'He burst out weeping' or 'He set to and wept' (14: 72). Both Matthew and Luke change this to the more natural phrase, 'He went out and wept bitterly' (Matt. 26: 75; Luke 22: 62).

(c) Mark's phraseology at times might give offence to Christian readers and Matthew or Luke have more acceptable phrasing. Both Matthew and Luke omit Mark's statement that some people thought Jesus was mad and that his friends (or his family) wanted to stop him from doing his work (3: 21). Mark bluntly states that at Nazareth Jesus 'could do no mighty work' (6: 5); Matthew changes this to, 'He did not do many mighty works' (13: 58). In Mark the rich man addresses Jesus as 'Good Master', to which Jesus responds, 'Why callest thou me good? None is good save one, God' (10: 18). Luke keeps this, but Matthew transfers the man's epithet 'good' to his question — 'What good thing shall I do?' — and makes Jesus reply: 'Why askest thou me concerning that which is good?' (Matt. 19: 17) and then continues, not very suitably, with Mark: 'One there is who is good'.

In other places the narrative in Mark implies criticism of the apostles. In the storm on the Lake they arouse Jesus with the reproach: 'Master, carest thou not that we perish?' (Mark 4: 38). Matthew has: 'Save, Lord; we perish' (8: 25) and Luke: 'Master, master, we perish' (8: 24). Mark says that James and John came to Jesus demanding the chief places by his side (10: 35); Matthew spares them by saying that their mother came with the request, although she immediately drops into the background and Jesus addresses his rebuke to the men themselves, as in Mark (Matt. 20: 20ff). Mark says that the disciples were 'sore amazed' when Jesus came to them in the boat on the Lake and explains their dullness by saying that 'their hearts were hardened' (6: 51–52). Matthew says, however, that they worshipped Jesus as the son of God (14: 33). It is plain to see in these and other instances that Mark has been altered to conform with the views of later writers and to avoid giving offence to readers. The reverse process is inconceivable.

(d) Mark's narrative of particular events is often the longest of the three and it is far more likely that the accounts in Matthew and Luke are shortened versions of Mark's than that Mark has expanded either of theirs. The dramatic conversation between Jesus and the father of the epileptic boy, with its description of his fits (Mark 9: 14-27) is briefly summarised in what we can only call Matthew's tame account (17: 14-18). Luke's is a better production (9: 38-42), but he also has omitted the central part of the story — the man's cry, 'If thou canst do anything . . .' and Jesus' rebuke. The stories of the demoniac (Mark 5: 1-20), of Jairus' daughter and the woman (5: 21-43) and the feeding of five thousand (6: 30-44) are all similarly shorter in the other two Gospels. In all these cases the others abbreviated Mark, but in doing so they deprived the story of much of its force and vivid character. The 609 verses in the whole of Mark which have parallels in Matthew are contained there in 523 verses, while the 357 verses of Mark in Luke become 325 verses.

The cumulative force of these arguments, based on extensive and exact study of the text of the three Gospels, has convinced scholars that Mark was the first of the Synoptic Gospels to be written. The reader will be able to notice further evidence for himself in studying the Gospels and comparing parallel passages.

In a copy of the New Testament the reader might indicate with a distinctive mark in the margin (say with differently coloured ink or pencil) the matter in

Mark which is reproduced in Matthew or Luke only or in neither. The following are the passages:

Markan matter found only in Matthew (i.e. omitted by Luke):

1: 5–6; 4: 33–34; 6: 1–6, 17–29, 45–56; 7: 5–31; 8: 1–21; 9: 10–13, 28, 43–47; 10: 1–10, 35–45; 11: 12–14, 20–22, 24; 13: 10, 18, 27, 32; 14: 26–28; 15: 3–5.

Luke omits Jesus' visit to Nazareth, the death of John the Baptist, the request of James and John, discussion with Pharisees about divorce and the withered fig-tree. These may be accounted for by his inclusion elsewhere of parallel matter from another source (see Luke 4: 16–30; 22: 24–27; 13: 6–9), while the Jewish discussion about divorce and the somewhat gruesome account of the Baptist's death were perhaps considered to have no interest for his Roman readers.

Luke also omits Mark 6: 45 to 8: 26. Here we may take each narrative in turn and see reasons why Luke should have omitted it. The account of the walking on the Lake (Mark 6: 45–56) is like the earlier story of the storm. The discussion about Jewish rules of purity (Mark 7: 1–23) would be meaningless for Gentile readers; the conversation with the Greek woman (Mark 7: 24–30), implying a limitation of Jesus' ministry to Jews, would not be acceptable to Luke; the cure of the deaf stammerer (Mark 7: 31–37) and the blind man (8: 22–26) might remind Romans of cures by physical means by Gentile magicians; the feeding of the four thousand is so much like the five thousand that it might well be disregarded (Mark 8: 1–10); the demand of the Pharisees for a sign and the warning against them (Mark 8: 11–21) would be pointless for Gentiles. If Luke, considering the writing of a fairly lengthy book (and his Gospel is the longest of the four, as it is), had to decide to leave out something, these are the very passages which he would be most likely to omit.

An alternative explanation is that of Streeter, who conjectured that the copy of Mark's Gospel which Luke had was defective. It was torn at 6: 47 (at the words 'and he alone') and resumed at 8: 27 (with the words 'he asked his disciples'). Hence Luke puts the story of Peter's confession (without mentioning Caesarea Philippi) immediately after the feeding of the five thousand, joining these two Markan verses in the words 'as he was praying alone, the disciples were with him; and he asked them . . .' (Luke 9: 18).[1]

Markan matter found only in Luke (i.e. omitted by Matthew):

1: 23–28, 35–38; 4: 21–24; 6: 30; 9: 38–41; 12: 41–44.

This matter is not of great importance. It includes two brief stories of healing from Mark 1, some short passages of teaching and the story of the widow's mites.

Markan matter without any parallel in Matthew or Luke:

1: 1; 3: 20–21; 4: 26–29; 7: 3–4, 32–37; 8: 22–26; 9: 29, 48–49; 13: 33–37; 14: 51–52.

This includes one parable (the growing seed) and two incidents (the healing of the deaf stammerer and the blind man at Bethsaida), apart from small sections of teaching and the incident of the youth in Gethsemane. The parable could have been omitted because

[1] See B. H. Streeter: *The Four Gospels*, pp. 176ff.

it is so much like the parable of the mustard seed (Mark 4: 30–32), which both Matthew and Luke reproduce. The two healing stories both have peculiar features which may not have endeared them to the other writers: Jesus employed material means (saliva was thought to have healing power) and with the blind man the cure appears to have been gradual.

All the rest of Mark's Gospel is found in both Matthew and Luke.

The fact that each of the two writers omits some passages from Mark and that about thirty verses of Mark are missing in both Matthew and Luke has given rise to the question: Was the book which was used exactly the same as our Mark? It has been suggested that there existed an earlier form of Mark's Gospel, called by German scholars *Urmarkus*, or Primitive Mark, which was shorter than our present book. But there is no direct evidence that such a book existed and it is not sound criticism to multiply, without very good grounds, hypothetical documents if one can explain the facts without them. The attempt to discover an *Urmarkus* has now generally been abandoned.

CHAPTER V

THE GOSPEL OF MARK

THE CONSTRUCTION OF THE GOSPEL

Mark's Gospel was probably the earliest attempt to set down an account of the life and work of Jesus in an orderly and systematic form. The main sources used by the writer were in all probability oral. He knew the episodes which we have classified as Pronouncement-stories, miracle-stories, biographical-sketches, and the teaching of Jesus which was reported among the early Christians. If some of it was already written down, it would probably be of a fragmentary character.

The material at his disposal was arranged by the author to form a 'book'. In making his selection of episodes and teaching, he put together material which had a similar subject or purpose. He thus gave an account of (a) activities connected with the opening of Jesus' ministry in Galilee (chapter 1); (b) stories of conflict with the Jewish authorities (2-3); (c) parables illustrative of Jesus' teaching (4); (d) acts of power (5); (e) the training of disciples (6) and journeys outside Galilee (7-9); (f) a journey to Jerusalem (10); (g) the last days in Jerusalem (11-16). This constitutes the Markan 'scheme' which, as we have seen, was largely followed by Matthew and Luke.

The Characteristics of Mark's Gospel

The writer made most use of the accounts of Jesus' activities. In this book there is an impression of speed and urgency. The writer is fond of the Greek word translated 'straightway' or 'immediately'. He goes from one incident to another with very little 'padding' in between. He crowds a large amount of activity into his very first chapter. He is fond of the historic present tense, using it 151 times in his narrative. The book opens without formal introduction, with an abrupt statement about John the Baptist, prefaced by what appears to be a kind of 'heading' — 'The beginning of the gospel. . . .' Jesus appears, without previous introduction, at verse 9. The style of the Greek is rough and the grammar sometimes faulty.

Mark presents **four** aspects of the life and person of Jesus:

(i) As a man of action and of mighty works. From the first, Jesus' authority is noticed by the people — in his words (1: 22) and in his deeds (1: 27; cf. 2: 12). The author seems to be answering, by anticipation, the question which Jesus' enemies put to him: 'By what authority doest thou these things?' (11: 28). Mark regards the powers of Jesus as a demonstration of his divine mission and his Messiahship.

(ii) As the Messiah. This is the 'heading' of the book (1: 1). The demons recognise this (1: 24, 34), but it is not known by men. They think of him only as John the Baptist or Elijah or a prophet (8: 28). Peter's acknowledgment at Caesarea Philippi (8: 29) marks a turning-point in the narrative. Jesus is first publicly proclaimed as Messiah by Bartimaeus at Jericho (10: 47). The Messiahship is hinted at on the occasion of his entry into Jerusalem (11: 9–10) but the first claim to that dignity by Jesus himself is at his trial, in answer to a question from the High Priest (14: 61–62). The book closes with the verdict of the Roman centurion, that this was 'a son of God' (15: 39) — meant by him no doubt in a pagan way but intended by Mark to be understood in the Christian sense.

(iii) As the Servant. After Caesarea Philippi (8: 31ff) Jesus speaks of a suffering Messiah, who serves and sacrifices himself for men. Three times there is a forecast of what will happen at Jerusalem (8: 31; 9: 31; 10: 33). The thought of the Messiah seems to be combined with the conception of the Suffering Servant, as pictured by Deutero-Isaiah, but the term used is 'Son of Man'; apart from 2: 10 and 2: 28 this term occurs only after Caesarea Philippi. There appears to be a definite reminiscence of Isaiah 53 in the words given in 10: 45, that 'the Son of Man came not to be served but to serve, and to give his life a ransom for many'.

(iv) As a teacher. Much of the teaching in Mark is given in connection with incidents or in answer to questions from disciples or enemies. Many of the Pronouncement-stories, ending with a saying of Jesus, are found in Mark. More specific and connected teaching is given in the parables in 4: 3–34, the sayings in 9: 41–50 and the apocalyptic chapter 13.

DIFFERENT VIEWS OF MARK'S GOSPEL

Students of Mark have shown great divergence in their views of the nature of the book and what it is intended to teach.

(i) One traditional way of regarding the Gospel has been to treat its outline as a reliable account, in detail,

THE GOSPEL OF MARK

of the ministry of Jesus, correct in its chronology and the order of events, preserving genuine reminiscence of the disciples. It is this outline which is followed in the main by the other two Synoptists. The 'Markan hypothesis', as it was called, sought to trace this definite 'scheme' in the account, as evidence of careful planning and exact reporting on the part of Mark.

In the Galilean period, Mark includes stories of Jesus' preaching, healing acts and opposition from his enemies which, in contrast to the general popularity, his words and works evoked. The 'Galilaean sunshine' was also clouded by misunderstanding. So Jesus chose twelve men to be with him and learn his secret and to go forth to preach his message. He had decided not to trust the great crowds but to concentrate on a few. On the return of these apostles from their mission tour, Jesus wished for retirement with them, but was frustrated by the crowds, when he crossed the lake, and was discovered even by a Greek woman in Phoenicia. So he proceeded to Herod Philip's territory and there, away from the crowds, the disciples reported on their work and on people's views about Jesus and Peter made his confession. Thereafter Jesus began to speak of a suffering Messiah and shortly afterwards the journey to Jerusalem (apparently the only one) commenced, leading swiftly to the final clash with the Jewish authorities there and the crucifixion.

There is admittedly much that is attractive in this view and it gives an intelligible and straightforward story of Jesus' ministry. It was generally assumed by the supporters of this view that this outline came from Peter, who was thus the writer's informant not only about particular incidents but also the general order of events throughout.

This view, however, has its difficulties. The Markan 'scheme' is incomplete and inadequate chronologically. There is little indication of the passing of time in Mark; the only mention of the seasons of the year is in the references to the ears of corn in 2: 23 and the green grass in 6: 39, both of which indicate the spring. But we have no clue whether it is the same spring or whether that was the year in which Jesus went to Jerusalem. If all the events in Mark's story happened within twelve months, is that enough for Jesus to have become known throughout Galilee and even for his fame to have reached Phoenicia (7: 24) and Jericho (10: 47)? Mark records only one visit to Jerusalem, whereas Q hints that he had more than once appealed to the city (Luke 13: 34; Matt. 23: 37: 'How often . . .'). This document also suggests an extensive ministry in places in Galilee which are either mentioned only once in Mark (e.g. Bethsaida: Mark 8: 22) or not mentioned at all (e.g. Chorazin: Luke 10: 13; Matt. 11: 21). When Jesus reaches Jerusalem, there is no indication in Mark how long it was before the Passion; the popular view of a 'Holy week' is based on the assumption that the entry into the city took place on a 'Sunday', but Mark does not say so. It might have happened some time before the Passover. The only indication of time in the Jerusalem period is the note that the plot against Jesus was hatched two days before the Passover (Mark 14: 1).

It is indeed perilous to rely upon Mark for an adequate or chronological outline of Jesus' work. It is doubtful if Mark would have been interested in this, even if he had been able to provide it. He was concerned to set forth a gospel — a proclamation of good news (1: 1). This is not to say that his outline of Jesus' ministry is unreliable. On the whole it presents a true historical picture of Galilaean work, healing and teaching, the opposition of his enemies, his journey to Jerusalem and the last days. But we must not claim for it more than the writer himself intended. It is going too far to conclude that the general 'scheme' of Mark represents a fully trustworthy and carefully worked-out account, covering all the incidents narrated, so that it is possible to say of an incident that it happened at a particular place at a particular stage in the ministry.

(ii) The Form Critics go to the other extreme and tend to regard Mark as a kind of patchwork, without the possibility of placing any reliability on its historical and geographical notices. It embodies the oral material which was in circulation in the early Church, but the writer had at hand only fragmentary and disconnected episodes. They hold that the connections between the paragraphs are entirely artificial, being the work of Mark himself, and are not to be depended on to give any reliable account of the situation or the connection between different incidents.

The truth in this view is that the Gospel is certainly a collection of episodes and there are abrupt transitions between one paragraph and another; sometimes there does seem to be little relation between consecutive paragraphs. But it is going too far to suggest that no reliance can be placed on the Markan arrangement. There is definite progression in Mark's account; the ministry of Jesus begins after his baptism by John and his temptations; his main work is done in Galilee; thence he travels to Jerusalem, where the opposition of the Jewish authorities reaches its climax. The writer is here surely following a tradition of the course of

Jesus' work, although in but general terms, and he has arranged his oral material within this historical framework.

The view of the Gospel as a series of disconnected episodes without any trustworthy or certain connection thus goes too far in the other direction, as a revolt against the rigidity of the 'Markan hypothesis'.

(iii) Mark is often regarded today primarily as a theological work. It is held by such critics that Mark did not intend to give an objective narrative of the life and work of Jesus; his book is neither a history nor a biography but is the writing of a theologian. The first attempt must be to understand his theological point of view; then his treatment of the story of Jesus becomes plain. A number of such recent views can only be summarised here:

(a) W. Wrede in 1901 (*Das Messiasgeheimnis in den Evangelien*) held that Mark's Gospel was written in order to expound a theory of the 'Messianic secret'. Faced with the fact that the early Christians proclaimed Jesus as the Messiah after the resurrection, Wrede said that this was their own invention and that Jesus was not accepted as the Messiah until then and did not himself claim to be the Messiah. The Gospel of Mark was written to account for the Christian proclamation, in face of Jesus' own silence. The writer held that Jesus was recognised as Messiah by the demons, and later by the intimate band of disciples, but he told them to keep this a secret until after the resurrection. The 'Messianic secret' was, however, so Wrede urged, an artificial construction, and the Gospel was the exposition of a theological view, not to be regarded as historically reliable.

(b) A different point of view was upheld by J. H.

Ropes, who regarded Mark's Gospel as 'a kind of theological pamphlet', which was written to explain how it was that the Messiah suffered death at the hands of his own people. 'The Gospel of Mark is a discussion of a theological problem in the form of a dramatic historical sketch.'[1]

(c) Others have held that the writer of Mark was a Paulinist and was concerned mainly to expound the views of the apostle to the Gentiles. Paul deals in Rom. 9–11 with the problem of the rejection of the Messiah; the counterpart of this teaching, so B. W. Bacon held, is the theory in Mark of the 'hardening' of the disciples' hearts (Mark 6: 52; 8: 17).[2] Loisy advanced this idea of Paul's influence on the writer of Mark to the extreme of holding that Paul himself is referred to in the 'outsider' with whose work the original disciples were not to interfere (Mark 9: 38–40) and the 'little one' who must be received in Jesus' name (Mark 9: 37).[3]

(d) A more recent attempt to understand Mark in this theological way is that of Austin Farrer, who holds that Mark's theological arrangement was cyclic. The narratives told in the early parts of the book 'prefigure' the later events of the Passion and resurrection. He hoids that this restores the unity of the Gospel and makes it 'a profoundly consistent, complex act of thought'. The book is consequently arranged not on an historical basis but artificially, as determined by 'motives of Christian symbolism'.[4]

The 'theological' view of Mark has arisen to a large extent as a reaction against the view that the book

[1] *The Synoptic Gospels*, p. 12.
[2] *The Gospel of Mark*, p. 144. *Is Mark a Roman Gospel?*, p. 80.
[3] *L'Evangile selon Marc*, pp. 279f.
[4] *A Study in St. Mark*, pp. 7, 146.

presented a 'simple human Jesus', and was to be treated as a straightforward biography. It does seem plain now that much of the arrangement of Mark's material is due to the writer himself and that doctrinal considerations did influence him in this. But one suspects that in some cases the critic is reading into Mark's narrative theological conclusions which he has himself reached on other grounds.

Another difficulty is that the critics are by no means agreed on what was the theological purpose of Mark and their views are often divergent and irreconcilable. There is much in the Gospel, too, which plainly has no connection with a theological purpose; many of the incidents are surely related simply because the writer thought it worth while to preserve them and to give them a more permanent form than they could ever have had in the oral period.

THE SOURCES OF MARK'S GOSPEL

In the case of Matthew and Luke, we have seen how we can trace the use of written sources. In the case of Mark the study is necessarily more uncertain and speculative, as there has not been preserved any previous attempt at the writing of a Gospel, of which Mark may have made use.

(i) One source was obviously the oral material which we have studied in chapter I. Many of Mark's narratives still bear the marks of the 'form' which they took when still being told by word of mouth. The study of Form-Criticism is generally concerned mainly with Mark's Gospel.

(ii) The oldest tradition about the authority behind Mark is contained in the words of Papias, who was

THE GOSPEL OF MARK

bishop of Hierapolis, in Asia Minor, about A.D. 130. As reported by Eusebius, the Church historian (about 325), Papias quotes 'the Elder' (or 'Presbyter') as saying: 'Mark, having become the interpreter of Peter, wrote down accurately all that he remembered of the things said and done by the Lord, but not however in order. For neither did he hear the Lord, nor did he follow him, but afterwards, as I said (attached himself) to Peter, who adapted his teaching to the needs (of the moment, or: of his hearers), but not as though he were drawing up a connected account of the Lord's sayings. So then Mark made no mistake in thus recording some things just as he remembered them, for he made it his one care to omit nothing that he had heard and to make no false statement in them.'

According to this statement, the authority behind Mark was Peter. The word 'interpreter' has sometimes been taken to mean that Mark translated Peter's words from one language to another — perhaps from Peter's Aramaic to the common Greek. It is, however, more likely that the word means rather a kind of secretary or one who sought to interpret Peter's ideas to others. If the writer is John Mark of the Acts, his relation to Peter might be the same as he had formerly had to Paul and Barnabas (Acts 13: 5).

Most students of Mark have concluded that there is Petrine matter in Mark and that the authority of the apostle lies in some measure behind the book. Peter is especially mentioned in such places as 1: 30; 9: 5; 10: 28; 11: 21; 16: 7 (apart from passages where he naturally plays a leading role).

The reference which Papias makes to Mark's 'order' has sounded to some students to be disparaging. Some have concluded that the Elder was comparing Mark's chronological scheme with some other 'order' in another book — perhaps the Gospel of Matthew or the Fourth Gospel, which certainly does give a different 'order' in several respects. Others have taken the word to refer rather to literary arrangement; in this case the comparison is more likely to have been with Matthew, where the author has arranged Jesus' teaching in particular in a more orderly fashion. P. Carrington, however, holding that Mark was compiled to provide lessons for reading in Christian services, considers that Papias was criticising Mark's calendrical order, as an arrangement of lections, because this could not be used, or could only be used with difficulty, in the Asiatic churches with which he was concerned.[1] It is, however, possible that all these views read too much into Papias' words and that he was referring in general terms to the lack of connection between incidents in the Gospel and the fact that the arrangement of similar material is not consistently carried through in the whole book.

(iii) Petrine matter does not, however, account for the whole Gospel. There are traits which do not suggest an eye-witness behind the narrative. There are two accounts of the feeding of a multitude (6: 34–44; 8: 1–10), which are generally considered to be variants of the same incident. This suggests that Mark had two different accounts, from more than one source; one may have been oral and the other written. The confusion which is shown in some places about the geography of Galilee and the north of Palestine in general also suggests that the writer had not at hand an eye-witness, to whom he could refer for more accurate details.

[1] *The Primitive Christian Calender*, pp. 58f.

(iv) It is probable that some written sources were used for the teaching of Jesus in Mark. The parables in 4: 3-34 may already have been written down and arranged in this fashion. There is a series of sayings in 9: 41-50, which are introduced by an incident (9: 38-40), but there is little connection between this and the sayings which follow or indeed between sayings which are here put together. The connecting links seem to consist of words which occur in contiguous sayings, such as 'name' (verses 39 and 41: see the R.V. margin for the literal rendering here), 'cause to stumble' (verses 42 and 43-47), 'fire' (verses 48-49) and 'salt' (verses 49-50). This suggests that the sayings were already collected and Mark simply copied them into his Gospel. Such a document would be somewhat like Q, although a quite independent collection.

It is probable also that a written document underlies chapter 13 or part of it. This chapter consists of teaching of Jesus said to have been given to the four chosen apostles, in answer to a question about the time of the destruction of the Temple (13: 1-3). But most of the chapter has little relation to this initial enquiry and consists of the 'signs' and other features which were common in apocalyptic thought and literature among Jews and Christians in the first century. It has often been thought that Mark was making use of a written document in this chapter, compiled by some Jewish-Christian writer. This 'Little Apocalypse', as it is called, may have consisted of verses 7-8, 14-20 and 24-27, which reflect the conventional apocalyptic outlook more than the rest of the chapter. To this some writer — perhaps Mark himself — added warnings which Jesus gave to the disciples about the treatment which they must expect from men and exhortations to watch for some coming crisis. The theory of the Little Apocalypse is not held now so rigidly as it was once; but it is still possible that verses 5–27 had already been compiled and were inserted by Mark into his narrative at this point.

(v) In recent years attempts have been made to distinguish a number of written sources, both for Mark's narrative matter and the teaching. Vincent Taylor draws attention to what he calls a number of 'small complexes' — groups of narratives in which there is a common theme or interest, such as the stories of cures in 1: 21–39, the conflict stories in 2: 1 to 3: 6, the parables in 4: 1–34, the statements about ritual cleanness in 7: 1–23 and the incidents on the journey through Perea in 10: 1–31.[1] Some of these may have already existed in written form before Mark included them in his Gospel.

A general conclusion, which would incorporate what is of value in many of the suggestions here considered, would be that Mark depended on the material circulating in the oral period, that he had the authority of Peter for much of what he wrote, that probably some of Jesus' teaching and quite possibly some narratives were already in written form, although fragmentary, and that no attempt had yet been made to set out in a systematic arrangement an account of Jesus' ministry from its beginning until the end. This study reinforces the pioneer nature of Mark's labours.

THE AUTHORSHIP OF MARK'S GOSPEL

The tradition of the early Church was that the book was written by one called Mark. This dates from the

[1] *The Gospel According to St. Mark*, pp. 90f.

time of Papias and there was never any real doubt among early Christians. The Mark who is thus named is taken to be the man who is called John Mark in the New Testament — Acts 12: 12, 25; 13: 5, 13; 15: 36–37; Col. 4: 10; 1 Pet. 5: 13; Phile. 24; 2 Tim. 4: 11.

(i) The style of the book, with its rough-and-ready mode of writing and its occasional lapses in grammar and phraseology, suggests one who was not a polished writer in Hellenistic Greek; he knew the language and could write quite forcefully in it, but it was not his native language. John Mark, who was presumably a native of Jerusalem, would have Aramaic as his mother tongue, although no doubt able to speak the common Greek which would be needed on his travels. But he would probably have occasionally to translate his thoughts, naturally expressed in Aramaic, into Greek. This would account for the presence of Aramaisms in the Gospel.

(ii) The writer was vague about the geography of northern Palestine and sometimes made confusing statements or actual mistakes. He often does not state which part of Galilee he is referring to (e.g. 6: 31) and the disciples wander to and from 'the other side' of the Lake in a very confusing way (6: 45; cf. 5: 1, 21). The disciples start from an unnamed place to go to Bethsaida (6: 45), but they arrive at Gennesaret (6: 53), which is quite a different district, and do not arrive at Bethsaida until considerably later (8: 22). In the meantime they have visited Phoenicia (7: 24) and made a journey by a quite incredible route to Decapolis (7: 31). Reference to a map will show that it is impossible to make a coherent account of these travels. The narrative suggests a writer who did not know northern Palestine well. John Mark would be more familiar with Judea and the neighbourhood of Jerusalem.

(iii) The book does not suggest the work of an eyewitness, although there are traits that suggest an eyewitness as one authority behind the narrative. The only place where there is a hint of personal presence is in the strange incident at Gethsemane told in 14: 51-52, where it has been suggested Mark himself was the 'young man'. If not, this may have been his informant about the prayer of Jesus. Peter could not have told Mark, for he was asleep.

(iv) The rough character of the book may also be regarded as according with the character of Mark as portrayed in the Acts — probably impulsive and somewhat unreliable, but sufficiently attractive to be defended by his cousin Barnabas and later to become reconciled to Paul himself. One would expect this John Mark to write a book such as this, with all its faults and yet its attractiveness and charm.

THE DATE OF MARK'S GOSPEL

If the book was written by John Mark, the date must obviously be in the apostolic era. An early Prologue to the Gospel says that it was written after the death of Peter. This is agreed by Irenaeus (about 185), who says that he wrote after the deaths of Peter and Paul — that he 'transmitted in writing the things preached by Peter'. Clement of Alexandria (about 200), however, says that he wrote while Peter was still preaching in Rome. Later tradition spoke sometimes as if he almost wrote at the dictation of Peter, but the general consensus agreed with the words of Papias, that Mark simply put down Peter's preaching without specifying when.

The date usually accepted now for the writing of the Gospel is between 65 and 70, for the following reasons:

(i) Peter and Paul were probably both put to death in the persecution under Nero, in 64–65. The death of his master was probably one of the reasons which impelled John Mark to take this work in hand.

(ii) There is a warning in the apocalyptic passage, 13: 14, of 'the abomination of desolation standing where he ought not'. (The phrase is literally 'the appalling horror' or 'profanation' and is quoted from Daniel and 1 Maccabees, where it refers to a heathen altar set up in the Temple court by Antiochus Epiphanes in 168 B.C.) The reference in Mark seems to be studiously vague, as if the writer were not sure what form the 'abomination' would take. A strange point of grammar is that he uses a masculine participle for 'standing', whereas the Greek word for 'abomination' is neuter. This suggests that he thought the climax of the apocalyptic 'signs' (all of which were to happen in that generation) would be the appearance of a personal evil force, such as the Jews spoke of under the name of Anti-Messiah or Anti-Christ. We know that this did not come about; but in 70 the Roman armies, after the capture of Jerusalem, entered the Temple courts and set the buildings on fire. If Mark had been writing after the fall of Jerusalem, he would surely, thinking of the Roman standards in the Temple, have used the correct neuter participle and would have been more definite — 'the abomination of desolation set up in the Temple', or some such phrase. This is what Matthew does (24: 15), writing later, while Luke boldly changes Mark's phrase to 'Jerusalem encompassed by armies' (21: 20). The vague phrases in Mark suggest that the final siege had not yet begun, but he feared the worst yet dared not be more definite about the horrors to come.

(iii) A note of persecution and suffering runs through many parts of the Gospel. Jesus warns his disciples about the need for taking up a cross (8: 34); the disciples must drink his own cup (10: 38f) and must learn to serve and suffer, following the example of the Son of Man (10: 45). They must learn not to be ashamed of him and his words (8: 38) and are promised ample compensation (10: 29f). The emphasis in such passages would be of special comfort to the Christians who were living in the shadow of persecution in the time of Nero.

(iv) A date towards the end of the first generation of Christians is most likely in view of the needs of the Church of that time. The reasons given in chapter I which led to the writing of a Gospel are particularly applicable to such a time.

The place of writing is generally taken to be Rome, although other places, such as Antioch and Alexandria, have been suggested. It is certain that Mark wrote for Gentile readers. When he quotes Aramaic words of Jesus, he translates them for their benefit (5: 41; 7: 11, 34; 15: 22) and goes out of his way to explain the Jewish practice of ritual-washing (7: 3-4). There are also a number of Latin words (in their Greek form) — such as legion (5: 9), denarius (12: 15), quadrans (12: 42), praetorium (15: 16) and centurion (15: 39) — but this is not decisive for Rome as the place of writing, as these words were regularly used in Hellenistic Greek. Early writers (Clement, Irenaeus) say the Gospel was written at Rome.

The Conclusion of the Gospel

In the Revised Version there is a space after the last words of Mark 16: 8 — 'for they were afraid' — and the margin indicates the doubt about the rest of the chapter. The evidence is overwhelming that the writing of Mark ends with these words:

(i) The oldest texts finish at this point. These include the Greek manuscripts, the Sinai and the Vatican codices, and the most trustworthy copies in Latin, Syriac, Armenian and Georgian versions. The copies used by Matthew and Luke also finished here.

(ii) In the majority of manuscripts verses 9–20 are given after verse 8. But early Church writers up to the end of the fourth century used Greek copies which did not contain this passage. Most manuscripts which do have it are late ones. The weight of the textual evidence is against the inclusion of verses 9–20 as part of Mark's Gospel.

(iii) This conclusion is borne out by an examination of the contents of the passage. It appears to be based on the accounts in other books. Luke's story of the walk to Emmaus and the appearance of Jesus in Jerusalem are referred to in verses 12 and 14–15, while verses 17–18 seem to reflect the adventures of disciples in the Acts; the reference to Mary Magdalene in verse 9 seems to come from John. As all these books were written later than Mark, this paragraph could not have been composed by that author.

(iv) Examination of the style and vocabulary bears out this conclusion. Both are quite un-Markan. One can sense even in an English translation how the graphic style of Mark is suddenly dropped at verse 8 and a smoother style is adopted, beginning with a reference to Mary Magdalene as if she has not been already mentioned.

This passage is evidently an early attempt to supply a suitable conclusion to the Gospel. An Armenian MS. written in the tenth century has a note above it — 'of the presbyter Ariston' — but this is probably a late guess by a scribe. We do not know who wrote verses 9–20.

(v) Another attempt was made to conclude the Gospel, which is found in some MSS. and versions — with or without verses 9–20. (These are called respectively the Shorter and the Longer Conclusions.) This short passage is printed in Moffatt's translation of the New Testament.

We are thus faced with a problem: How did Mark's Gospel originally end? Why was it thought necessary to supply these later 'Conclusions'? The problem is accentuated by the fact that, in the Greek, verse 8 finishes with a conjunction (*gar* — the Greek word for 'for'). This word could be used to end a sentence or even a paragraph (as it does sometimes in the Greek version of the Old Testament), but would seem to be a very abrupt ending of a book. There are two possible answers:

Some scholars think that Mark did finish his Gospel here, with the women running from the tomb in fear and keeping silence about what they had seen and heard. It is held that such an ending is thoroughly Markan. The message of the Gospel ends, as it began (1: 22–27), on a note of astonishment and awe. There was no need for Mark to tell of resurrection appearances of Jesus, for these were well known. The climax of the 'good news' is the proclamation: 'He is risen' (16: 6).

Other scholars insist that a Gospel could not have ended on such an unsatisfactory note. Earlier in the

THE GOSPEL OF MARK

book the writer has hinted at an appearance in Galilee (14: 28; 16: 7) and he would not cease his work until he had recounted this. Streeter suggests that the lost ending of Mark was the document which lay behind the story of the incident in Galilee told in John 21.

These are hence a number of possibilities of what happened to the rest of Mark's account:

(i) The writer may have been interrupted before he could set down anything further. Perhaps he intended to revise and complete his work but could not. He may have died. Such an occurrence has not been unknown in the history of literature; Charles Dickens left the MS. of *Edwin Drood* on his desk one night but died in his sleep, leaving the book unfinished.

(ii) Some think that the conclusion of the book, written by Mark and telling of Jesus' appearance in Galilee, was deliberately suppressed because it conflicted with accounts in Luke and John of appearances in Jerusalem and its neighbourhood. But Matthew's Gospel tells of an appearance in Galilee and the ending of that book was never suppressed.

(iii) The conclusion may have been accidentally lost. If the early form of the Gospel was a papyrus roll, the end of the long sheet would get worn through constant reference and might easily fall off. If the original was a codex, the last page or so might become detached. Streeter suggests that an early copy, if not the very original, was torn in some riot against the Christians in Rome.

Whether the words at 16: 8 were those originally intended by Mark as the conclusion of his book or not, the abrupt conclusion is in keeping with the abrupt opening of the Gospel and the rugged and dramatic nature of this first written proclamation of the Gospel.

CHAPTER VI

THE NON-MARKAN MATERIAL IN MATTHEW AND LUKE

WE NOW reach the next stage in the solution of the Synoptic Problem. The matter in Matthew and Luke which can be attributed to Mark accounts for over one-half of Matthew and over one-third of Luke. When we proceed to examine the non-Markan matter in these two Gospels, we are faced with further phenomena which require explanation.

NON-MARKAN PARALLELS IN MATTHEW AND LUKE

There are passages in these two books which are parallel in substance and language. Study of these prompts the question: whence did the writers obtain this material?

(i) This matter consists of about 200 verses. There are 171 verses in Matthew which are closely parallel to 151 in Luke. In addition there are over 90 verses in Matthew which have partial parallels in 94 verses in Luke. Remembering the use made of Mark as a source by the other two writers, we are led to ask: Is this another case of a common document?

(ii) In these passages the verbal agreement is often

close. A very striking instance is the parable of the mote and the beam:

MATTHEW 7: 3-5.	LUKE 6: 41-42.
3 And why beholdest thou the mote that is in thy brother's eye, but considerest not the beam that is in thine 4 own eye? Or how wilt thou say to thy brother, Let me cast out the mote out of thine eye; and lo, the beam is 5 in thine own eye? Thou hypocrite, cast out first the beam out of thine own eye; and then shalt thou see clearly to cast out the mote out of thy brother's eye.	41 And why beholdest thou the mote that is in thy brother's eye, but considerest not the beam that is in thine 42 own eye? Or how canst thou say to thy brother, Brother, let me cast out the mote that is in thine eye, when thou thyself beholdest not the beam that is in thine own eye? Thou hypocrite, cast out first the beam out of thine own eye, and then shalt thou see clearly to cast out the mote that is in thy brother's eye.

Other passages, which may be similarly set out and studied, are:

The teaching of John the Baptist:
  Matthew 3: 7-10. Luke 3: 7-9.
The temptations of Jesus:
  Matthew 4: 1-11. Luke 4: 1-12.
Teaching on anxiety:
  Matthew 6: 25-33. Luke 12: 22-31.
On confessing Christ:
  Matthew 10: 32-33. Luke 12: 8-9.
The message of John the Baptist from prison:
  Matthew 11: 2-19. Luke 7: 18-35.
The thief in the night:
  Matthew 24: 43-44. Luke 12: 39-40.

This verbal agreement again suggests a common source. As with the passages taken from Mark, the similarities are too detailed and subtle to be accounted for simply by oral tradition.

(iii) This common matter often follows the same order in the two Gospels. Each of them has a large section of Jesus' teaching (the Sermon on the Mount in Matthew 5-7, the Sermon on the Plain in Luke 6: 17-49). Both of these begin with Beatitudes and finish with the same parable; within the section the sayings on judging others and the parable given above are followed by warnings about a tree as known by its fruit and the parable of the two foundations. In both Gospels the Sermon is followed by the story of the centurion's servant (Luke 7: 1–10; Matt. 8: 5–13. Matthew inserts the Markan story of the leper first). These facts suggest not only that the section of teaching in the two accounts was in this order in a common source but also that the story of the centurion followed. Shortly afterwards, in both Gospels, there comes the account of the message of John the Baptist from prison (Matt. 11: 2–19; Luke 7: 18–35).

The conclusion drawn from a close study of all this common material is that here also Matthew and Luke were using a written document. This source has not, however, like Mark's Gospel, been preserved, so its existence must necessarily be hypothetical to a certain extent. It appears first to have been given the name of *Quelle* (German for 'Source') by Johannes Weiss in 1881, and the designation 'Q' is now generally used to indicate this matter common to Matthew and Luke but not found in Mark, or the document which contained this matter.

THE CONTENTS OF Q

This common matter consists mainly of teaching. At least two narratives — the centurion's servant and John's message from prison — were included. The following passages are assigned to Q by Streeter. The order is that found in Luke (since he reproduces Mark's order better, it is probable that he is more to be relied on in the case of Q also).

John the Baptist and Jesus' baptism: Luke 3: 2-9, 16-17, 21-22. (Matt. 3: 7-12, 16-17.)

Jesus' temptations and beginning in Galilee: Luke 4: 1-16a. (Matt. 4: 1-11.)

The Great Sermon: Luke 6: 20-49. (Matt. 5: 3, 4, 6, 11, 12, 15, 18, 32, 39, 42-48; 6: 19-34; 7: 2-5, 7-11, 16-27.) Many of these Matthaean passages, however, have parallels in other places in Luke, as shown below.

The centurion's servant: Luke 7: 1-10. (Matt. 8: 5-10, 13.)

John's question and Jesus' opinion of John: Luke 7: 18-35. (Matt. 11: 2-11, 16-19.)

Would-be disciples: Luke 9: 57-60 (possibly 9: 51-56, 61-62). (Matt. 8: 19-22.)

The mission of disciples: Luke 10: 2-16, 21-24. (Matt. 9: 37-38; 10: 10-13, 16; 11: 25-27; 13: 16-17.)

Jesus' defence against the Beelzebub charge: Luke 11: 9-52. (Matt. 7: 7-11; 12: 22-27, 38-45; 5: 15; 6: 22-23; 23 (passim).)

Warnings against fears and cares: Luke 12: 1b-12, 22-59. (Matt. 10: 26-33; 12: 32; 6: 19-21, 25-33; 24: 43-51; 10: 34-36; 5: 25-26.)

Parables of the mustard seed and the leaven: Luke 13: 18-21. (Matt. 13: 31-33.)

Sayings about entrance into the Kingdom: Luke 13: 22-30. (Matt. 7: 13; 8: 11-12.)

The lament over Jerusalem: Luke 13: 34-35. (Matt. 23: 37-39.)

Warnings to disciples: Luke 14: 11, 26-27, 34-35. (Matt. 10: 37-38; 5: 13.)

The Law and divorce: Luke 16: 13, 16-18. (Matt. 6: 24; 11: 12-13; 5: 18, 32.)

Warnings against stumbling-blocks, etc.: Luke 17:

1–6, 20–37. (Matt. 18: 6–7, 15, 21–22; 17: 20; 24 (passim).)

Possibly three parables where the parallels are not so close:

The Great Supper (or Marriage Feast): Luke 14: 15–24. (Matt. 22: 1–10.)
The Lost Sheep: Luke 15: 3–7. (Matt. 18: 12–14.)
The Pounds (or Talents): Luke 19: 12–27. (Matt. 25: 14–30.)

In the reader's copy of the Gospels there might now be indicated, by colours in the margin, the Q matter in Matthew and Luke.

The contents of Q might be classified as follows:

(i) John the Baptist and the baptism and temptations of Jesus.
(ii) The teaching of Jesus to his followers — warnings against fears and anxiety, against causing stumbling; the charge to the disciples when they were sent out on their mission.
(iii) Parables — the mustard seed and the leaven; possibly others.
(iv) Jesus' conflict with his opponents; sayings about the Jewish Law; warnings to would-be disciples.
(v) Two narratives — the centurion's servant and John's message from prison.

The material from Q contains many of Jesus' references to the countryside and the processes of nature. It portrays the more human side of Jesus' personality and work. There is little about Judaism or teaching that would be of special interest to Jewish disciples. This suggests that Q was compiled for a church which was largely Gentile. This may have been Antioch, where, according to the Acts of the Apostles (11: 20), the first preaching was made to the Greeks.

It is probable that Q was compiled before Mark's Gospel and so it is one of the earliest writings of the Church. But it would be a mistake to regard it as a complete Gospel. There is no suggestion, for instance, that Q contained an account of the Passion. The matter in Matthew and Luke which we may assign to Q ceases when Jesus reaches Jerusalem.

It is, however, probable that Q was longer than we can gauge simply from the parallel matter in Matthew and Luke. Some of the passages which are peculiar to either may well have come from Q but ignored for some reason by the other writer. Thus Matthew has Jesus' reply to two would-be disciples (8: 19–22), found also in Luke (9: 57–60). But Luke adds a reply to a third man (9: 61–62), which may well have been in Q also. Of Matthew's parables of the Kingdom of God in chapter 13, two are assigned to Q (the mustard seed and the leaven), for they are paralleled in Luke, but possibly the parables of the treasure and the pearl-merchant (Matt. 13: 44–46) were also taken by him from Q. If we may judge from their use of Mark, it is very unlikely that either writer made use of the whole of Q and quite probable that one of them has reproduced it more fully than the other.

THE ORIGINAL FORM OF Q

As stated above, the order of the Q passages in Luke is more likely to be nearer the original than in Matthew.

Luke also tends to reproduce blocks of Q matter, whereas Matthew conflates his sources, mixing up Markan material with Q and other matter. In considering the question of the original wording of Q, we must bear in mind the free way in which both the other two writers treated Mark, Matthew abbreviating and sometimes omitting quite vital matter in a narrative and Luke rewriting Markan passages in his own style. It is probable that they treated Q in much the same way. It seems sometimes as if one writer and sometimes the other gives the original words.

The question has also been raised whether Q was originally compiled in Aramaic, the language in which Jesus spoke. If it was, it is probable that it had already been translated into Greek by the time it was used by Matthew and Luke, although it is possible that the two did not use the same Greek rendering. This may account for some of the divergences in their wording.

We thus see that we cannot regard Q as a rigid documentary source in quite the same way as Mark's Gospel, as used by Matthew and Luke. It was not a full 'Gospel', published and circulated as a complete account of the work of Jesus. Attempts have been made in recent years to dispense with Q as a separate source and to account for this non-Markan matter by the theory that one writer made use of the other's book. This attitude has arisen as a protest against a too rigid view of Q. It cannot satisfactorily account for all the phenomena in such parallel passages as are set out on pp. 83–85, which clearly point to dependence on a common source. But some of this matter may not have yet been authoritatively committed to writing and we may use the term Q as a convenient designation for a tradition of Jesus' teaching which was known

NON-MARKAN MATERIAL IN MATTHEW AND LUKE 89

to Matthew and Luke, much of it written but some of it possibly still in the oral stage.

MARK AND Q

There are some places where Mark and Q overlapped. There are about forty verses in Mark which are also found in a similar form in Matthew and Luke where (as can be seen particularly clearly in Luke) the context is Q matter. Hence we are justified in assigning them to Q as well as Mark. The passages in Mark which are thus paralleled are:

Mark 1: 4–8: John the Baptist's preaching.
Mark 1: 9–13: The baptism and temptation of Jesus.
Mark 3: 22–30: The accusation of Jesus' enemies.
Mark 4: 30–32: The parable of the mustard seed.
Mark 6: 7–11: The mission of the twelve disciples.
Mark 12: 38–40: Warning against the scribes.
Various short sayings: 4: 21 (the lamp); 8:12 (the demand for a sign); 8: 34 (taking up the cross); 8: 38 (being ashamed of Christ); 9: 42 (on causing to stumble); 9: 50 (on salt); 10: 11 (divorce); 11: 22–23 (on faith); 13: 21 (false Messiahs).

The question inevitably arises: Did Mark make use of Q? Opinion on this question has been divided among scholars, but it is generally concluded today that Mark did not know of or did not use Q. If this document had been available to him, he would surely have reproduced not merely these few short passages but more of the teaching of Jesus. The wording in Mark and Q also is not generally near enough to suggest Mark's use of the same source as Matthew and Luke in these places. The occurrence of passages in both Mark and Q indicates that some of the teaching of Jesus was remembered and written down independently in different places. The fact that both Mark and the compiler of Q (and subsequently the writers of Matthew and Luke) included these particular passages is an argument for their dependability as genuine teaching of Jesus.

When we have extracted from Matthew and Luke the Markan material and the passages taken from Q, we are still left with a considerable amount of matter found only in the one Gospel in each case. This matter is generally designated, for convenience, M and L respectively.

Matter Peculiar to Matthew

This consists of 282 verses. In addition, there are about 90 verses which have partial parallels in Luke. The matter peculiar to Matthew consists of narratives, of additions made to the Markan account and of teaching of Jesus.

(i) Narratives found only in Matthew are: The genealogy of Jesus and stories of his birth and infancy (chaps. 1–2), the healing of two blind men (9: 27–31; this, however, seems to be a conflation of Mark 8: 22–26 and 10: 46–52), the coin in the fish's mouth (17: 24–27), the end of Judas (27: 3–10), the guard at the tomb (27: 62–66; 28: 11–15), the resurrection appearance in Galilee (28: 16–20).

(ii) The main additions to the Markan narratives are: The hesitation of John at the baptism (3: 14), Jesus' preaching in Galilee, with an Old Testament quotation (4: 13–16), teaching in the incident in the cornfields (12: 5–7), healing by Jesus, with an Old Testament quotation (12: 15–21), the people's question about Jesus as Son of David (12: 23), Peter's attempt to walk on the water (14: 28–31), additions to the story of the Greek woman (15: 22–25), the praise and promise to Peter at Caesarea Philippi (16: 17–19), details in the story of the entry into Jerusalem, including an Old Testament quotation (21: 4–5), healing and praise of Jesus in the Temple (21: 14–16), Judas' reply at the Last Supper (26: 25), Jesus' words at his arrest (26: 52–53), the warning of Pilate's wife (27: 19), Pilate's hand-washing (27: 24–25), the earthquake at the crucifixion (27: 51–53), the descent of an angel and an earthquake at the tomb (28: 3–4).

(iii) The teaching of Jesus found only in Matthew consists of:

Sections of the Sermon on the Mount (5: 7–10, 13–24, 27–30, 33–48; 6: 1–18; 7: 13–23).

Parts of the charge to the disciples (10: 5–8, 23–25, 40–41).

Most of chapter 23 (Woes on the Pharisees and scribes).

Ten parables: The tares (13: 24–30, 36–43), the hidden treasure (13: 44), the pearl merchant (13: 45–46), the drag-net (13: 47–50), the unforgiving servant (18: 21–35), the labourers in the vineyard (20: 1–16), the two sons (21: 28–31a), the man without a wedding garment (22: 11–14), the ten maidens at the wedding (25: 1–13), the sheep and the goats (25: 31–46). There are three parables which have partial parallels in Luke: the lost sheep (Matt. 18: 12–14), the marriage feast (22: 1–10), the talents (25: 14–30).

Various sayings: 9: 13a; 11: 28; 12: 5–7, 11–12; 13: 52; 15: 22b–24; 18: 15–22; 19: 28.

Much of this M material gives Matthew's Gospel its distinctive tone. The narratives are characterised by references to angels and dreams as means of divine revelation, and there is a tendency to heighten the miraculous and the marvellous. Quotations from the Old Testament and Jewish phrases are inserted into the narrative, sometimes quite unsuitably. Matter relating to Peter is added to Mark's accounts. Some of the material raises suspicions as to its historicity and borders on the apocryphal.

The teaching of Jesus in M brings out the Jewish element in the gospel, in Jesus' attitude towards the Law and the anti-Pharisaic tone of many of the sayings. There is an interest in eschatology and judgment and an emphasis on the Church.

Matter Peculiar to Luke

This consists of about 490 verses. It comprises both narrative and teaching.

(i) The narratives found only in Luke are: The stories of the birth of John the Baptist and Jesus (1: 5 to 2: 40), the incident of Jesus' boyhood (2: 41–52), the genealogy of Jesus (3: 23–38), the rejection at Nazareth (4: 16–30), the call of Peter (5: 1–11), the widow's son at Nain (7: 11–17), the anointing in Simon's house (7: 36–50), the women who accompanied Jesus (8: 1–3), the Samaritan village rejection (9: 51–56), a would-be disciple (9: 61–62), the return of seventy disciples (10: 17–20), Mary and Martha (10: 38–42), the healing of an infirm woman (13: 10–17), the plot of Herod (13: 31), the healing of a man with dropsy (14: 1–6), the healing of ten lepers (17: 11–19), the meeting with Zacchaeus (19: 1–10), the lament over

Jerusalem (19: 41–44), a quarrel at the Last Supper and words to Peter (22: 24–34), the trial before Pilate (in some details) and Herod Antipas (32: 1–25), the weeping of the Jerusalem women (23: 27–31), the two crucified criminals (23: 39–43), the walk to Emmaus (24: 13–35), the appearance of Jesus in Jerusalem and the ascension (24: 36–53).

(ii) The teaching matter found only in Luke consists of: Various sayings: 4: 25–27 (Jesus' address at Nazareth); 12: 13–15 (warnings about riches); 13: 1–5 (the Galilaeans and the Siloam tower); 13: 31–33 (Jesus on Herod); 14: 7–14 (on inviting to a banquet); 16: 14–15 (on the Pharisees); 22: 24–30 (on greatness and service); 23: 34, 43, 46 (sayings at the crucifixion). Other passages, not attributable to Jesus: 1: 1–4 (the dedication to Theophilus); 3: 10–14, 15, 17 (John the Baptist's teaching).

There are fourteen parables peculiar to Luke: The two debtors (7: 41–42), the good Samaritan (10: 30–37), the friend at midnight (11: 5–8), the foolish rich man (12: 15–21), the fig tree (13: 6–9), the tower builder (14: 28–30), the king going to war (14: 31–32), the lost coin (15: 8–10), the prodigal son (15: 11–32), the unrighteous steward (16: 1–12), the rich man and Lazarus (16: 19–31), the slave and his master (17: 7–10), the unjust judge (18: 1–8), the Pharisee and tax-collector (18: 10–14). Three parables have a partial parallel in Matthew: The great supper (14: 15–24), the lost sheep (15: 3–7), the pounds (19: 12–27).

As in the case of Matthew, it is here also that this special matter gives the characteristic tone to the whole Gospel. The narratives show an interest in women, in outcasts and Samaritans and in Roman officials.

The teaching of Jesus emphasises prayer, the Spirit of God, women and outcasts.

The matter peculiar to each Gospel could be marked in the reader's New Testament with a special colour for each. If matter from Q has already been marked in a distinctive way, the sections in Matthew and Luke without any indication will be those taken from Mark.

THE FORM OF THIS MATERIAL

In view of the previous study of Mark and Q, as well as the researches of the Form-Critics, the question arises: Was the matter peculiar to one Gospel taken from a written source or did the writer simply reproduce the oral material in these passages? It is difficult to say with certainty in either case.

(a) In the case of Matthew's M matter, one of the sources was probably a collection of Old Testament passages, already arranged in writing. At points in his narrative he introduces these, sometimes suitably but frequently in a forced and artificial way. This suggests that he did not quote these direct from the Old Testament (and some of them do not agree in wording with either the Hebrew or a Greek version) but made use of a collection of passages which had already been compiled.

The way in which the teaching in Matthew is arranged also frequently suggests the use of a written document — for instance the five examples of Jesus' attitude to the Law (5: 17-48) and the three instances of Jewish religious observance (6: 1-18). Similarly the three parables of judgment in chapter 25 may already have been arranged in this way in written form. Some of this arrangement may, however, be due to the skill of the writer himself, as in the case of the five discourses of Jesus in his Gospel (see pp. 110f).

The narratives peculiar to Matthew were probably oral traditions which circulated in a Jewish Christian environment. They are mostly fragmentary in nature — details about Peter or Pilate or Judas which the writer thought fit to introduce into his account; there is little extended continuous narrative, apart from the birth-stories of chapters 1 and 2. Some of the matter introduced into the Markan narratives consists simply of editorial comments.

(b) Luke's peculiar narrative matter may have been written down beforehand or may be oral stories which he himself heard. If the author was the companion of Paul, who stayed with him at Jerusalem and Caesarea (Acts 21–26), the latter is more likely. But if the author was a later writer, it is more likely that he found written accounts of at least some of these stories. In either case, he re-wrote them in his own Greek style.

The teaching peculiar to Luke consists mainly of parables; the sayings enumerated above are often given in connection with parables or incidents. One feature of the Lukan parables is that they are placed in a particular setting in many instances and sometimes have a fairly long narrative introduction — e.g. the two debtors (7: 36ff), the good Samaritan (10: 25ff), the foolish rich man (12: 13ff), the lost sheep and coin (15: 1ff), the pounds (19: 11ff). Sometimes the Lukan setting seems somewhat artificial and the parables could well stand by themselves; for instance, by the time the third of the parables of the 'lost' is reached (15: 11ff), the original situation in 15: 1–2 has been lost sight of. These facts suggest that at least in some cases the parable may have existed separately, perhaps in a written collection, and has been placed in this setting by Luke.

Summary

B. H. Streeter enunciated a 'Four-document hypothesis' — an extension of the two-document theory of the use of Mark and Q — by which the story of Jesus is seen to rest not upon three independent Synoptic writers, but upon four early sources or traditions. It may be represented by this diagram:

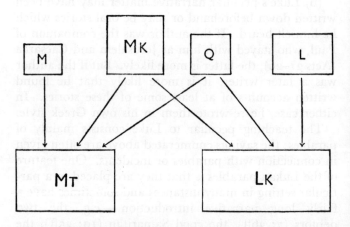

Our modern principles may be shocked at first by the suggestion that the writer of a Gospel made use of an earlier work, without acknowledging his debt. But we must remember that this was the accepted practice in ancient times. The Old Testament writers, in the historical and prophetic books, adopted this. Greek historians used sources and this practice was also followed by the Jewish historian, Josephus, in his accounts of the Jewish history and the war with Rome. There was no 'copyright' for books and no convenient signs like inverted commas or footnotes, by which a writer might show that he was quoting. An author in the first century would feel quite at liberty to make use of the work of another, sometimes copying out a paragraph with very little alteration and at other times rewriting the whole in his own style. Both these methods can be illustrated from the use of their sources by the three Synoptic evangelists.

CHAPTER VII

THE CHARACTERISTICS OF THE TEACHING OF JESUS

THE NAME by which Jesus in the Synoptic Gospels is most frequently called is that of 'Teacher' or 'Rabbi'. (This is somewhat obscured in the A.V. and R.V., as the Greek word *didaskalos* is sometimes rendered 'Master'.) He is said in the Gospels to be teaching more frequently than preaching. This is in accordance with Eastern methods. The religious teacher was a familiar figure in the Eastern world, and indeed still is, in India and other places. He has generally no settled home but travels from village to village or town to town. He depends upon the willing hospitality of the people for his maintenance and they are glad to give him support even out of their poverty. He has a company of disciples whom he instructs in his doctrine and whom he sends out to teach in his name. The function of Jesus as a teacher would therefore be one which his contemporaries in Palestine would appreciate.

Sometimes Jesus taught in the synagogue of a town or village (e.g. Mark 1: 21, 39; 6: 2). In the Jewish synagogue the elder who was in charge of the worship might invite any member of the congregation to read from the roll of the Law or the Prophets and to give a comment on it. Jesus appears to have taken this part in the service on a number of occasions. But much of his teaching was delivered on far less formal occasions

— in private houses, at the meal table and most frequently in the open-air. Much of it was given not in formal address but in answer to a question or a difficulty put to him by an enquirer. This may seem to us to be a rather casual method of teaching, but it is typical of the East. Eastern peoples are neither so used to nor so fond of the set discourse, lecture or address as we tend to be in the West.

In addition to this general manner of teaching, we notice that Jesus adopted certain specific methods which are also typical of the East and especially of Palestine in the first century. Four of these methods can be seen in the Gospels.

I. *Proverbs or aphorisms*

The wisdom of the East consists in pithy sayings, which sum up a great truth. The Old Testament has many examples of these and one book — Proverbs — consists of a collection of such aphorisms. Many of Jesus' sayings have become so familiar as to be considered proverbial. One instance is the Golden Rule (Luke 6: 31; Matt. 7: 12). Another is the statement that he who exalts himself shall be humbled, but he who humbles himself shall be exalted (Luke 18: 14; Matt. 23: 12). A saying which occurs in Mark and also in the Q matter was probably frequently on Jesus' lips: 'He who finds (or saves) his life will lose it and he who loses it will find (or save) it' (Mark 8: 35; Matt. 10: 39; 16: 25; Luke 9: 24; 17: 33). This appears to be a contradiction and is deliberately put in this way, to make people think out what it really means. A pithy statement like this is remembered far better than our general phrases about the value or efficacy of self-sacrifice.

In some cases the eastern aphorism is a deliberate exaggeration and may even seem, if taken literally, to depict an impossible or even absurd situation. This method also was adopted by Jesus, to awake people's minds and get them to think out his meaning. Thus he spoke of the impossibility of the higher life for a man who trusts in his riches and put it in one epigram: 'It is easier for a camel to go through a needle's eye than for a rich man to enter the Kingdom of God' (Mark 10: 25). This is a graphic eastern way of saying 'It can't be done!'

II. *Pictorial language*

This last example illustrates a second method which Jesus adopted — the use of word-pictures. Whereas we often tend to think and speak in abstract forms, the easterner thinks in pictures. There are examples of this in literature from the East in all ages, from Old Testament times to the present day. As prosaic statements of fact, some of Jesus' sayings seem impossible and even absurd. But if we see them as word-pictures, much of the teaching in the Gospels becomes illuminated.

Thus, in criticising the proud, religious Pharisee, Jesus did not simply say in general terms that he had no sense of proportion. He put it in a brilliant word-picture — that of the 'blind guides', who 'strain out the gnat and swallow the camel' (Matt. 23: 24). It is a picture of the Pharisee preparing to drink; he makes sure, by means of a filter, that he has got rid of the smallest impurity — and then does not notice that he is drinking a huge camel! Another striking word-picture is that of the man who finds fault with other people but is blind to his own greater faults.

Jesus put it in the parable of the Mote and the Beam — the man wishes to remove a speck from his brother's eye, when he himself has a great beam of wood in his own! (Luke 6: 41-42; Matt. 7: 3-5).

Akin to this use of pictorial imagery is Jesus' adoption of the method used by some prophets in the Old Testament, of acting his teaching. Thus to instil the lesson of humility he took a child and set him in the midst of the disciples (Mark 9: 33-37). To show he came in peace and not as a conquering Messiah, he deliberately chose an ass on which to ride into Jerusalem (Mark 11: 1-11). To impress on his disciples at the Last Supper that his body was to be mutilated and his blood shed, he broke a piece of bread and poured out wine before them all.

III. *Poetry*

This may seem surprising at first to some, for as printed in our New Testaments the teaching of Jesus does not look like poetry. This is because we associate poetry with rhyme and rhythm and expect to see it printed in short lines. Poetry among the Jews, however, often had neither of these characteristics. The Old Testament abounds in poetry, not only in the book of Psalms, which is a collection of religious poems. The book of Job is a long epic poem, with a prose introduction and conclusion. The Old Testament prophets often delivered their utterances in poetic form.

The characteristic of such Hebrew poetry is not necessarily rhythm (although this was often used) or rhyme (which was infrequent) but repetition. The poet makes a statement and then repeats the same thought in a slightly different form. Sometimes the second statement completes the meaning of the first (e.g. Ps. 24: 1: 'The earth is the Lord's, and the fulness thereof; The world, and they that dwell therein'). Sometimes the second statement is the negative of which the first line is the positive form (e.g. Prov. 6: 20: 'My son, keep the commandment of thy father, And forsake not the law of thy mother'). These, with many other varieties, are different forms of what is called parallelism — that is, parallel statements which express the same thought. (Those who wish to study further examples are referred to the following passages: Job 23: 2-5; Ps. 1: 1-2; 37: 1-12; Prov. 15: 1-9; Isa. 10: 1-4; 60: 1-2.)

Much of the teaching of Jesus is poetry of this type. It is possible that in the original Aramaic, in which Jesus would speak to his disciples, some of his sayings possessed rhythm, which would enable them to be remembered the more easily. This has, of course, been lost in the Greek of the Gospels, but parallelism in ideas and phrases may still be discerned, in any translation. (In Moffatt's New Testament such passages are printed so that this may be seen — e.g. in Matt. 5-7 and 10, and Luke 6 and 11.)

The following are some examples of poetic parallelism in Jesus' teaching (the passages are quoted from the Revised Standard Version):

Matthew 7: 7-9:

> Ask, and it will be given you;
> Seek, and you will find;
> Knock, and it will be opened to you.
> For everyone who asks receives,
> > And he who seeks finds,
> > And to him who knocks it will be opened.

Here the first line has two parts — the injunction to ask, and the result. The second line has the same two parts and expresses exactly the same thought. So does the third line, in the same form. These three lines are thus parallel. Then there follow another three lines, each of which corresponds to a line in the first set. Thus there are here six different ways of saying the same thing and yet the effect is not monotonous.

The four lines which follow are similarly parallel:

Matthew 7: 10:
> Or what man of you, if his son asks him for a loaf,
>   will give him a stone?
> Of if he asks for a fish,
>   will give him a serpent?

'Loaf' corresponds to 'fish', 'stone' to 'serpent'. At the same time there is an antithesis, and this is brought out in the final lines of the poem:

Matthew 7: 11:
> If you then, who are evil,
>   Know how to give good gifts to your children,
> How much more will your Father who is in heaven
>   Give good things to those who ask him?

'You' is parallel and yet contrasted with 'your Father', 'good gifts' with 'good things' and 'your children' with 'those who ask him'.

Matthew 7: 16–18:
> Are grapes gathered from thorns,
>   or figs from thistles?

Every sound tree bears good fruit,
> but the bad tree bears evil fruit,
A sound tree cannot bear evil fruit,
> nor can a bad tree bear good fruit.

Here the second line is parallel with the first. In the last four lines there is a double parallelism. A positive statement ('sound tree — good fruit') is followed by its negative counterpart ('bad tree — evil fruit'). These two lines together are then repeated, but the ideas are crossed over! The 'sound tree' of the first is related to the 'evil fruit' of the second and the 'bad tree' of the second is connected with the 'good fruit' of the first.

Matthew 6: 25:
> Do not be anxious about your life,
>> what you shall eat or what you shall drink,
> Nor about your body,
>> what you shall put on.
> Is not life more than food,
>> And the body more than clothing?

Here line one is amplified by line two. Line three is amplified in line four. Lines five and six sum up the whole poem, repeating again the terms of lines one and three.

Luke 6: 27:
> Love your enemies,
>> Do good to those who hate you,
> Bless those who curse you,
>> Pray for those who abuse you.

'Love your enemies' is explained by the parallel:
'Do good to those who hate you,' just as blessing those
who curse means praying for those who abuse. This is
a good example of the way in which the meaning of
Jesus' teaching becomes plainer when we realise the
form which he adopts. People have declared that his
precept to love our enemies is impossible and absurd.
This poem explains what Jesus meant by this admittedly difficult saying. 'Love' does not mean a sentimental attitude of abstract affection, but active goodness
— doing good to one's enemies and seeking their welfare.

Matthew 7: 24–27:
>   Everyone who hears my words
>   and does them
>   Will be like a wise man,
>   who built his house upon the rock.
>   And the rain fell
>   and the floods came
>   and the winds blew
>   and beat upon that house,
>   But it did not fall,
>   because it had been founded on the rock.
>
>   Everyone who hears my words
>   and does not do them
>   Will be like a foolish man,
>   who built his house upon the sand.
>   And the rain fell
>   and the floods came
>   and the winds blew
>   and beat against that house,
>   **And it fell,**
>   **And great was its fall.**

This is a poem of two stanzas, which concludes the Sermon on the Mount. When it is set out in this way, we can see at once the parallelism, here not between words and phrases, but between two whole stanzas. Each line in the second stanza corresponds to a line in the first. At the end, however, there is a sudden break. One can imagine Jesus' hearers expecting him to conclude: 'because it had been founded on the sand'. But there is a dramatic drop into prose — 'and great was its fall'. This is well expressed in Moffatt's version: 'And down it fell — with a mighty crash'.

This parable is found also in Luke 6: 46–49. Luke, however, has paraphrased it and made the poem into a piece of prose. It is generally concluded that the passage came from the document Q, the wording of which is probably given more faithfully in Matthew.

Other examples of Jesus' poetic teaching may be examined in Matthew 5: 13–14; 6: 19–21; 7: 13–14; Mark 9: 43–48.

IV. *Parables*

We naturally associate parables with the Gospels, thinking of this as Jesus' distinctive method. But this form of teaching was not invented by him. Jewish Rabbis spoke to their pupils in this way and there are two or three instances of parables in the Old Testament.

The word parable is derived from two Greek words — *para* ('by the side of') and *ballo* ('I put'). A parable is thus a comparison between two things which are placed alongside. Parables must not be treated as fables or as allegories. A fable is a purely imaginative tale, told in order to point a moral, which is generally appended to it in a rather artificial way. An allegory is an elaborate narrative in which each person or thing represents somebody or something in another sphere or in everyday life. Some fantastic attempts have been made to interpret the parables of Jesus as elaborate allegories and in the process they have lost their vitality and reality and have been made to mean things which Jesus never intended and to apply to situations which he never envisaged. It is hence fatal to stress every detail in a parable. It is a broad comparison in which one aspect of God's kingdom or character or man's conduct is stressed.

A parable is not intended to express a general ethical truth (like a fable) or to give a detailed description of a spiritual situation (like an allegory); its intention is rather to stir the minds of the hearers or the readers, to awake them to the recognition of a particular situation and to challenge them to action. In many of Jesus' parables it is essential to bear in mind the religious and political situation of the time, for they were spoken to Jews of the first century, not to twentieth-century westerners. They were an attempt to awake Jesus' contemporaries to the realities of their own situation, its possibilities and its dangers; only after we have seen how they apply to that situation can we consider how they might apply to ours.

Jesus' parables are of two types. Some are true comparisons, which generally relate to the Kingdom of God. Many of them begin: 'The Kingdom of God is like . . .' Something in the world of nature or of men is compared with the Kingdom of God or the character of God himself. In chapter 4: 1–34, Mark has collected a series of such parables about the

Kingdom. The writer of Matthew took this section and reproduced it, adding other parables from Q or from his own special source, and so compiled chapter 13. Each parable is intended to stress one aspect of the Kingdom of God. It is in some way like a lamp, a seed, a mustard-seed, a farmer, leaven, treasure, a pearl-merchant, a net.

In addition to these parables which are strictly comparisons, there are other passages which are generally called 'parables' in popular speech but are rather of the nature of illustrative stories. Here Jesus seeks to portray some praiseworthy feature of human conduct or thought or holds up some human failing as a warning. These stories are found almost exclusively in Luke — the parable of the Good Samaritan, portraying neighbourly conduct (Luke 10: 30–35), the Rich Foolish Man (12: 16–20), the Prodigal Son (15: 11–32), the Pharisee and the Tax-collector, stressing the need for humility in prayer (18: 10–13). In such parables people are held up as examples to follow or, sometimes, to avoid. There is no strict comparison. Here also it must be emphasised that these should not be treated as allegories.

We may notice the realms from which Jesus draws his images, both in the parabolic and pictorial sayings and in the parables. They are mainly concerned with the life of everyday people — features of the countryside, such as the sower (Mark 4: 3), fishers (Matt. 13: 47–48), sheep and goats (Matt. 25: 32; Luke 15: 4) or of home life — a woman in her house (Luke 15: 8–9), making bread (Matt. 13: 33), a man waking his neighbour (Luke 11: 5), children playing at their games (Matt. 11: 16; Luke 7: 32) — or from men's work and social relations. All these were things which would be familiar to his hearers. Jesus' images are not far-fetched analogies but deal with the stuff of the everyday lives of his fellow men.

These preliminary considerations will be borne in mind as we turn to the two Gospels which contain most of the Synoptic teaching of Jesus, before studying in detail various aspects of that teaching.

CHAPTER VIII

THE GOSPEL OF MATTHEW

THE CONSTRUCTION OF MATTHEW'S GOSPEL

The basis of the narrative and the general order of events in this Gospel are Mark's account. The writer has produced what has been called a revised edition of Mark. After his introductory stories in chapters 1 and 2, he follows the Markan order, without deviation, to the end of chapter 4. Chapters 5-7 consist of teaching material from other sources. Then he resumes the Markan narrative (Matt. 8-12), with some variations in the places of events. (See p. 54.) From chapter 14 onwards the Markan story is followed, with no variation.

Into this Markan framework the writer has inserted material from other sources. He adds to the narrative, quoting the Old Testament and inserting additional information (see pp. 90f). The main departure from Mark is his insertion of blocks of Jesus' teaching. There are five such discourses: the Sermon on the Mount (chapters 5-7), the charge to the twelve apostles (chapter 10), parables (chapter 13), discussion of the relations between disciples (chapter 18) and apocalyptic teaching and parables of judgment (chapters 24-25). Each discourse concludes with a similar formula, such as 'When Jesus had finished these sayings...' (7: 28; 11: 1; 13: 53; 19: 1; 26: 1).

THE GOSPEL OF MATTHEW

Each of these discourses has been compiled by the writer's method of conflation; he puts together matter from different sources to form an ordered section of teaching on a particular topic. Thus the Sermon on the Mount is composed of Q matter (also in Luke 6: 20-49, where Jesus delivers the teaching from a 'level place' — the Sermon on the Plain), other matter taken from Q (found also in Luke 12: 22ff and other places in Luke) and considerable matter from the source M. The charge to the twelve in chapter 10 is based on Mark 6: 7ff conflated with a similar charge in Q (found in Luke 10: 1ff), with sayings taken from Mark 13, Mark 9, M material and Q (cf., for example, Luke 13: 49-53). The chapter of parables (13) has as its basis Mark 4, to which the writer has added parables taken from Q (the mustard seed, although here conflated with the Markan version, and the leaven) and his own special source (the tares, the drag-net, the treasure and the pearl merchant). Chapter 18 consists of Q and M matter, with one section (verses 8-9) from Mark 9. The apocalyptic chapter 24 is based on Mark 13, with matter inserted from a similar apocalypse found in Q (Luke 17: 22-37).

The Characteristics of Matthew's Gospel

From the book itself we can conclude the chief interests of the writer and see what aspects of the life of Jesus he wished to enforce.

(i) There is an interest in Judaism and the Jews. This shows itself in four main ways:

(a) There is frequent reference to and quotation from the Old Testament. The writer employs a formula such as 'Then was fulfilled that which was spoken by the prophet . . .' or he says that something happened 'in order that it might be fulfilled which was spoken by the prophet . . .' Some of his references are inexact (the 'quotation' in Matthew 2: 23 cannot be traced in the Old Testament at all) and many of them are applied to events which they certainly never foresaw (the quotation from Hosea in 2: 15 is an historical statement about the Exodus from Egypt; the passage in Jeremiah, in Matthew 2: 17-18, referred to the Jews' going into exile in Babylon; the quotation from Isaiah in 1: 23 did not refer to the Messiah). He introduces Old Testament references to account for Jesus' residence at Capernaum (4: 12-16), for his counselling silence on those whom he cured (12: 15-21) and for his speaking in parables (13: 34-35). His attachment to the literal meaning of a passage leads to a ludicrous result in 21: 2-7, where, not appreciating the parallelism of the Hebrew, where the ass is obviously the same as the colt, he makes Jesus send for two animals and ride into Jerusalem upon both of them. In a somewhat similar vein, Jesus is referred to, sometimes in quite inappropriate places, as Son of David (12: 23; 15: 22; 21: 9).

(b) Christianity is regarded as the fulfilment of Judaism. In the Sermon on the Mount Jesus five times repeats an old Law, in order to expound the new and deeper meaning which he gives to it (5: 21-48). Jewish religious observances are assumed to be still in force among Jesus' disciples (6: 1-18). The word 'righteousness' is used to describe the Christian life (5: 20; 6: 1). Only in Matthew is this word, which is at the root of Jewish religion, found on the lips of Jesus.

(c) There is an anti-Jewish tone about the book, in spite of this. The writer particularly emphasises the failure of the Jewish religious leaders. Pharisees and Sadducees are 'lumped together' in an uncritical fashion. John the Baptist denounces them (3: 7; cf. Luke 3: 7, where his words are addressed to the people simply) and they come together to test Jesus by demanding a 'sign' (16: 1; cf. 16: 6). The bitterest tirade against Pharisees and scribes in any first-century Christian literature is in Matthew 23, and many critics, both Jewish and Christian, feel that Jesus' attitude was not so extreme as it is here depicted. The parable of the two sons (Matt. 21: 28-32), obviously directed against the Jews, is found only in this Gospel.

(d) The work of Jesus is portrayed as confined to Jews. The twelve disciples are expressly told not to go to Samaria or Gentile countries (10: 5). Although Mark had written that Jesus went to Phoenicia and entered a house and met a Greek woman (7: 24-25), this writer makes her 'come out from those borders' to meet Jesus (15: 22), who declares that he is not intended for such people (15: 24). This limitation lasts only until the resurrection. In the final paragraph of the Gospel Jesus commissions the disciples to preach to all nations (28: 19).

(ii) There is an interest in eschatology and the apocalyptic elements of Jesus' teaching. References to this in Mark are often heightened. The statement in Mark 9: 1 about the 'coming of the Kingdom with power' is interpreted to mean the coming of the Son of Man (Matt. 16: 28). The question of the disciples about the destruction of the Temple (Mark 13: 4) is altered to refer to Christ's 'coming and the consummation of the age' (Matt. 24: 3). The writer adds to Mark's reference to the appearing of the Son of Man (13: 26-27) conventional apocalyptic 'signs' such as the mourning of the earth's inhabitants and a great trumpet to summon the elect (24: 30–31). Throughout this chapter Matthew relates everything to the Son of Man's 'coming' (the Greek word *parousia*, frequent in Paul, occurs in the Gospels only in Matthew).

This characteristic is especially discernible in the M matter. This includes the parables of the tares and the drag-net, to which eschatological explanations are added which seem to be out of tune with the parables themselves (13: 24–30, 37–40, 47–50), the parable of the maidens at the wedding, with its exhortation to watch (25: 1–13) and of the judgment (or the sheep and the goats) (25: 31–46). Five times Matthew reproduces the conventional apocalyptic phrase, 'There shall be the weeping and gnashing of teeth' (13: 42, 50; 22: 13; 24: 51; 25: 30) and the term 'the consummation of the age' (mistranslated as 'the end of the world') occurs five times (13: 39, 40, 49; 24: 3; 28: 20).

(iii) The miraculous element is heightened. In Mark's story of the fig-tree near Jerusalem, Peter notices on the day following Jesus' words that it has withered (11: 20). Matthew makes it wither 'immediately' after Jesus speaks (21: 19). The madman in the country of the Gerasenes (Mark 5: 1–20) becomes two madmen with demons (Matt. 8: 28ff) and Bartimaeus at Jericho (Mark 10: 46–52) is likewise duplicated (Matt. 20: 29ff); a very similar story of two blind men is told in 9: 27. Miraculous signs are introduced — an earthquake and rending of the rocks, the opening of tombs at the crucifixion (27: 51–53) and a 'great earthquake' and the descent of an angel to roll away the stone of the tomb at the resurrection (28: 2–4).

(iv) There is a strong ecclesiastical interest. The word 'church' occurs in the Gospels only in Matthew — in words to Peter at Caesarea Philippi (16: 18) and in teaching on the settling of disputes (18: 17). In a number of places the writer seems to have in mind the conception of a Christian community. The book was probably written so that, among other uses, it could be employed as a manual of instruction for people who were being received into the Church; its arrangement of Jesus' teaching would facilitate easy reference. It has been suggested that the writer's intention was to supplement Mark, so that a book would be available which would be adequate for public reading in the services of the Church.[1]

THE AUTHORSHIP OF MATTHEW'S GOSPEL

From the book itself we should never conclude that it was the work of one of the original apostles of Jesus.

(i) The basis of the book is not the reminiscences of an eyewitness or apostle but is Mark's Gospel, which was itself written by one who was not an apostle.

(ii) The treatment of Mark's Gospel shows that the writer is one stage further removed from eye-witnesses. He alters Mark's narrative in ways which make the account less vivid and realistic, considerably abbreviating the Miracle-stories and altering the words of Jesus or his disciples in ways which show the influence of later reflection (see pp. 57f). His account is sometimes confused because of a misunderstanding of Mark's words: Mark describes two occasions in 16: 1-2 — the women bought spices after the end of the Sabbath (on Saturday after 6 p.m.) and went to the tomb

[1] G. D. Kilpatrick: *The Origins of the Gospel according to St. Matthew.*

early Sunday morning; Matthew mixes the two and so produces an impossible note of time (28: 1).

(iii) The author is out of touch with the historical and religious situation in Palestine in the time of Jesus. He makes a Greek woman (whom he calls, by perhaps a deliberate anachronism, a Canaanite) address Jesus as Son of David, a Jewish Messianic title (15: 21). He puts together Pharisees and Sadducees, in spite of their great differences and mutual enmity (3: 7; 16: 1, 6).

(iv) The additions and alterations made to the Markan narrative are improbable in themselves. It is not likely that the crowd thought that Jesus was the Messiah at an early stage in the ministry (12: 23). It is more probable that James and John came to Jesus demanding the chief places than that their mother asked for them, as Matthew says, and that Jesus entered Jerusalem sitting on one animal and not on two. Matthew says that Jesus healed the blind and the lame in the Temple court at Jerusalem (21: 14) but it is more probable that his last act of healing was that performed on Bartimaeus at Jericho, as Mark reports; the situation in Jerusalem was quite different. All these instances betray the hand of a later writer, not an eyewitness.

(v) The narratives which are peculiar to this Gospel[1] constitute the least trustworthy of all the strata which go to the making of the Synoptics. The birth-stories (1–2) conflict with Luke's account of the circumstances of Jesus' infancy. The additions to the Passion story are doubtful — the dream of Pilate's wife, his washing of his hands, the manner of Judas' death, the sealing and guarding of the tomb — while the accounts of the earthquake and resurrection of the saints at the cruci-

[1] See pp. 90f.

THE GOSPEL OF MATTHEW

fixion and the descent of the angel at the resurrection border on the stories which are found in the apocryphal Gospels, where the tendency is always to heighten the marvellous with such details.

All we would conclude from the Gospel itself is that the writer was a Jewish Christian. He had often been compared to the scribe who is mentioned in Matthew 13: 52. He sought to present Jesus to the Jews as the Messiah and Son of David, making use of 'things old and new'. He wrote probably for Jewish Christians, seeking to show how the events were 'fulfilments' of Old Testament prophecies; he thought of Christianity as a new Law and the Christian Church as the new Israel. In this way he showed that Judaism had been superseded.

THE WORDS OF PAPIAS ABOUT MATTHEW

In early Christian tradition the book was ascribed to Matthew the apostle. This opinion was probably derived from some words of Papias. In addition to his statement about Mark, he reports the Elder as saying: 'Matthew arranged (or composed) the oracles (Greek: *logia*) in the Hebrew language and each one interpreted them as he was able'.

Almost every word in this short sentence requires investigation. (a) In the second word the Greek MSS. differ. Some have 'arranged' or 'put in order' (*synetaxato*), while others have 'wrote' or 'composed' (*synegrapsato*). (b) 'Hebrew' without doubt means Aramaic — the popular language of Palestine, a Syriac dialect which was written in Hebrew characters. The classical Hebrew in which the Old Testament was written was not used among Jews then except in the Scripture readings in the synagogues and a popular translation had to be made into Aramaic in Palestine and into Greek in foreign countries. (c) The word *logia* means 'oracles' or 'sayings' — not quite the same as the usual word for 'sayings' or 'words', which was *logoi* (plural of *logos*). (d) The word 'interpreted' may mean 'translated' or may indicate application or interpretation or explanation.

Regarding the meaning of Papias' words, there are four possibilities:

(i) He may have meant our Gospel of Matthew. This was evidently the view among early Christian writers. It is possible that the Elder (if the reading 'arranged' — *synetaxato* — is the right one) was contrasting Matthew's Gospel, with its orderly arrangement of Jesus' teaching, with Mark's, which he criticised on account of its lack of 'order' (*taxis*).

If Papias did mean our Gospel of Matthew, it is clear that he made a mistake, both in attributing it to the apostle and in thinking it was written in Aramaic. Our Gospel does not show any signs of being a translation from Aramaic. It was written in Greek and at least one of the sources used by the writer — the Gospel of Mark — was a Greek work which we still possess. The other main source — the document Q — was probably also in Greek. We can only hazard a guess why Papias should have attributed the Gospel to the apostle Matthew. Perhaps it was because he noticed that Levi the tax-collector (Mark 2: 14) is called Matthew here (Matt. 9: 9); the title of tax-collector is also given to Matthew in the list of apostles (Matt. 10: 3; cf. Mark 3: 18). It was evidently assumed that Matthew was the same as Levi, by the writer of this Gospel (although this is not at all certain), and so the name of Matthew became attached to it, probably as a consequence of Papias' words.

(ii) Papias may have been referring to an Aramaic Gospel, which is now lost. We know that there was a Gospel of the Hebrews and a Gospel according to the Nazarenes. Papias speaks of a number of attempts to translate the *logia*: perhaps he thought that the Greek 'Matthew' was one translation of one of these Aramaic books.

The alternative to these two views is that he did not mean a Gospel, but one of the sources of our Gospels:

(iii) He may have meant a collection of Old Testament texts. Paul uses the word *logia* when speaking of his Bible — 'The oracles of God'. There is evidence that the first Christian written works were collections of passages, which have been called books of 'Testimonies'; they demonstrated ways in which, so the Christians thought, the Old Testament prophets and other writers bore testimony to the coming of Jesus. The apostle Matthew may have compiled such a collection (although one would hardly expect a former tax-collector, if he were one, to be interested in this). Papias' phrase, 'each one interpreted them as he was able' might then mean that each Christian preacher or teacher applied the Old Testament texts as he thought suitable. One Gospel of Matthew may have been one such attempt, for it is characterised by constant reference to the Old Testament.

(iv) The *logia* may have been a collection of sayings of Jesus. Streeter thought that it consisted of 'prophetic oracles' uttered by Jesus. Many have assumed that it was the document Q. It may have been the sayings which we call M, for these are often Judaistic in tone. Both the Q and M material were probably originally in Aramaic. On this view, the 'oracles' of Jesus were arranged or written down by Matthew, first in Aramaic. This is contrasted by Papias with the Gospel of Mark, which was not written 'in order' and did not make any attempt to 'give a connected account of the Lord's oracles'.

Against this view, however, is the fact that the sayings of Jesus were known among the early Christians as *logoi*, not *logia*.

In the case of the last two interpretations of Papias' words, the name of Matthew would have become attached to the Gospel because the writer used the *logia* compiled by Matthew, as a source.

We have to conclude that at present we do not know for certain what Papias meant. Many scholars incline today to the view that he did mean our Greek Gospel, but made a mistake both in thinking that it was originally written in Aramaic and in considering it was the work of Matthew. They point out that Papias is not a very reliable authority; Eusebius himself, who reports his words, says elsewhere that he was 'a man of small intelligence'. The tendency in some quarters at least is to discount his testimony and to consider it as merely a curiosity of early tradition.

The Date of Matthew's Gospel

The following considerations help to a conclusion about this:

(i) It is obviously later than Mark, which we may fairly certainly date between A.D. 65 and 70.

(ii) The language used in 22: 6–7 (an intrusion into the parable of the marriage feast) suggests that the writer knew of an occasion when a ruler did destroy those who ill-treated his servants and 'burned their city' — the destruction of Jerusalem by the Romans in A.D. 70 would immediately come to the mind of a Jew. The addition of the word 'desolate' in 23: 38 (in Luke 13: 35, the word does not occur in the Greek) points in the same direction — that the writer knew of the desolation of Jerusalem and the Temple. So does his alteration of Mark's vague phrase, 'the abomination of desolation standing where he ought not' (Mark 13: 14), to 'standing in the holy place' (Matt. 24: 15).

(iii) A date considerably after the actual events is suggested by the phrase 'to this day' (paralleled in Old Testament accounts written a good time after the events) — in the naming of the 'field of blood' (27: 8) and the story about the stealing of the body of Jesus (28: 15). The lack of distinction between Jewish parties, already noted (3: 7; 16: 1, 6) suggests that it was no longer valid when he wrote. The Sadducees as a party ceased to exist with the destruction of the Temple in 70.

(iv) There are suggestions in the book that the hope of the Parousia (the return of Christ) had grown dim and the author sought to revive it. He assured his readers that the Son of Man would come before the missionaries had finished their work (10: 23). He adds the word 'immediately' to the Markan source in 24: 29, intending to tell his readers that the 'signs' were imminent.

(v) The teaching about the treatment of erring brethren (18: 15–17) suggests the discipline of an ordered Christian community and the way in which 'false prophets' are referred to (7: 15ff) suggests dangers within the Church which were to be found towards the end of the first century (cf. 1 John 4: 1ff; 2 John verse 10). The instruction to the disciples to administer baptism in the name of the Trinity (28: 19) is also indicative of a late date, for the evidence in the Acts shows that the early practice was to baptise converts 'in the name of Jesus' (Acts 2: 38; 10: 48; 19: 5).

(vi) The legendary nature of much of the M narrative (see above, pp. 91f) also suggests a considerable lapse of time for such matter to develop.

For these reasons the date usually assigned to Matthew is A.D. 85 or some time later. Various places of writing have been suggested. It was obviously written in a place where Jewish Christians predominated, and so was not produced at any centre in Europe. The most likely place is somewhere in Syria — perhaps Antioch — or further east, in northern Assyria.

CHAPTER IX

THE GOSPEL OF LUKE

The Construction of Luke's Gospel

As with Matthew, the general order of events in Luke follows the Markan outline. In no major instance does the writer alter the sequence in Mark, although he does omit considerable sections. These have been enumerated and discussed above (see pp. 59f).

Luke's material consists of Q and L, in addition to Mark. He does not conflate these sources, as Matthew does, but gives blocks of Markan and non-Markan matter. It is thus easier, if a scheme of different colours has been used to mark the Gospels as suggested, to see at a glance what source Luke is following in any passage. Where matter overlaps, he sometimes omits one account. Instances will occur below. But he occasionally reproduces similar matter from two sources. Thus he gives two accounts of the charge to the disciples — in 9: 1ff (from Mark 6: 7–13) and in 10: 1ff (from Q) — and two apocalypses — in 21: 5ff (from Mark 13) and in 17: 20ff (from Q).

The Gospel is accordingly built on this plan:

Chapters 1–2: Birth-stories of John and Jesus (L).
  3: 1 to 4: 30 — from Q and L.
  4: 31 to 6: 11 — from Mark 1: 21 to 3: 6.
  6: 12 to 8: 4 — from Q and L.

8: 5 to 9: 50 — from Mark 4–6 and 8–9.
9: 51 to 18: 14 — from Q and L.
18: 15–35 — from Mark 10.
19: 1–28 — from L.
19: 29 to 22: 13 — from Mark 11–13.
22: 14 to 24: 53 — from L, with matter from Mark 14–16.

The L matter is listed on pp. 92f.

Luke's Method of Construction

This outline makes it plain that there are considerable sections of Luke which have no Markan matter in them. What procedure did Luke adopt, in thus alternating Markan and non-Markan matter? There are two views about this:

(a) That Luke based his Gospel on Mark, as did the writer of Matthew, and introduced into the Markan outline the material taken from Q and L. He did this in an orderly fashion, keeping the sections separate. In two big sections (6: 12 to 8: 4 and 9: 51 to 18: 14) he abandoned his Markan outline, to return to it after he had incorporated this Q and L matter. These passages have consequently been called the Lesser and the Greater Interpolations respectively, for they are considered as non-Markan interruptions of the Markan account. In the story of the Passion and trial of Jesus he also followed the Markan outline but introduced several distinctive features from L, which was here either a separate written source or consisted of oral material.

(b) That Luke first combined the Q and L material and added Markan passages later. In this case the basis of his Gospel is not Mark but the non-Markan sections. It is held that there was a 'First Draft' of

THE GOSPEL OF LUKE

the Gospel, before the writing of the book as we have it now, which did not contain any Markan matter. This theory of its composition is called the Proto-Luke hypothesis and was first put forward by Streeter in 1921, was fully expounded by him in *The Four Gospels* (1924) and developed by Vincent Taylor in *Behind the Third Gospel* (1926).

Proto-Luke consists of the following passages: 3: 1 to 4: 30; 6: 12 to 8: 4; 9: 51 to 18: 14; 19: 1–28; 22: 14 to 24: 53. The birth-stories (chapters 1--2) are not included, as it is thought that these were added to the completed Gospel; the dedication to Theophilus (1: 1–4) was added last of all, before publication.

The main arguments for this theory are as follows:

(i) Luke begins his Gospel, not with Markan matter, but with material from L and Q (3: 1ff). This opening, with its elaborate dating, reads indeed like the beginning of a book. The end of the Gospel similarly consists of his own distinctive matter (24: 13–53). This suggests that the author thought of his non-Markan matter as the framework of his book, into which he inserted Markan matter.

(ii) The QL sections read like a complete book — a Gospel in itself. There are here most of the essential parts of the story — John the Baptist's preaching, the baptism of Jesus and the temptations, his teaching at Capernaum and Nazareth, his healing, his treatment of sinners and outcasts, the journey to Jerusalem, the treatment of Samaritans and would-be followers, the sending out of the disciples to preach, teaching about prayer and riches and eschatology; and the trial of Jesus and his appearances after the resurrection. On the other hand, the Markan passages in Luke do not read like a connected story; they are interpolated into the non-Markan framework.

(iii) Where there are parallel narratives in the two sources — Mark and Q or L — Luke prefers the non-Markan. Thus he gives the accusation of Jesus' enemies that he was using the power of Beelzebub, from Q (Luke 11: 14-22), ignoring the Markan account (Mark 3: 22-30). Quite early in his Gospel he gives the story of Jesus' rejection at Nazareth (4: 16-30), so he does not reproduce the account from Mark 6: 1-6 when he reaches that point in the Markan narrative. In 7: 36-50 he gives the story of Jesus' being anointed by a woman in Galilee; so when he comes to the Markan account of an anointing at Bethany (Mark 14: 3-9) he omits it. In reproducing chapter 1 of Mark he leaves out one small paragraph, about the call of the first disciples (Mark 1: 16-20), but substitutes his account of the call of Peter (Luke 5: 1-11). He omits the request of James and John, with Jesus' teaching about service (Mark 10: 35-45), for he gives similar teaching in Jesus' words at the Last Supper (Luke 22: 24-27). In each case he rejects the Markan story and keeps the non-Markan. These facts suggest that he had already written this before he came across or incorporated Markan matter.

(iv) This view explains why the Markan matter is in solid 'blocks'. It suggests that this was a later addition to a book already written or at least drafted. Luke's treatment is in marked contrast to Matthew's, where the writer evidently had both Mark and Q before him and used them simultaneously, conflating both with his special traditions (M).

Streeter suggested that Proto-Luke was composed while Luke was staying at Caesarea with Paul. The record shows an interest in the Herod family and in Samaritans, and Caesarea was a port through which Galilaeans and Samaritans both passed. If this theory is correct, it means that we have another valuable early witness to the Gospel story, alongside of Mark, written possibly before this first of our Gospels.

This theory has not received unanimous support from New Testament scholars and there are those who hold that Luke used Mark as the basis of his book or put together Markan and non-Markan matter alternately as he wrote. They think that the QL material does not form a complete story and would be inadequate as the presentation of the Gospel; there are certainly big gaps in it. It contained, for instance, no account of the conflict between Jews and the authorities in Jerusalem. The weakest part of the argument is indeed that relating to the L passion story (Luke 22: 14 to 23: 56). Vincent Taylor answers that there were considerable Markan 'interpolations' made in Proto-Luke, before he issued the final Gospel. But if these later Markan additions are removed, there seems little of a connected account left; the Markan passages, though small in size, seem to act like the mortar which holds the bricks together and without this the structure collapses. And in many places in the later chapters, Mark seems to be the basis — in the story of Gethsemane (Luke 22: 39–53), Peter's denial (22: 54–62), the crucifixion (23: 33–38), the death and burial (23: 44–56) and the empty tomb (24: 1–12).

Is it possible that Proto-Luke should be considered to extend only to 19: 28 and that for the rest of his book Luke conflated Mark 14–16 with traditions and matter from L?

The Interests of Luke

The author of this Gospel was a Gentile, if the traditional ascription is to be accepted; and apart from this, his writing seems to show it. His book is the most literary of the four and indeed of any New Testament writing. He shows by his opening words that he can write in good classical Greek, for the dedication (4: 1–4) is as impressive in the Greek as in the English version; and he can suddenly change to a swift narrative in a style which recalls the Greek LXX (1: 5 to 2: 39). Some of his peculiar matter is written in fine style in Hellenistic Greek — the Prodigal Son (15: 11–32) and the walk to Emmaus (24: 13–35) — and some of his sentences have a dramatic quality which is equal to the best in contemporary Latin and Greek authors (e.g. 23: 25).

The author was especially concerned to show the origin of Christianity and to trace its progress throughout the Roman world. He had in mind readers like the Theophilus to whom he dedicated his two books (Luke 1–4; Acts 1: 1); there is no doubt that the same man penned both works. His writings have been called 'the first Christian apology'; this was the name given to writings which appeared later, addressed to Roman officials or even to the Emperor, to defend Christianity against its enemies and to show that it was not hostile to the State or dangerous to society. Thus we find in the Gospel:

(i) The elements in Jesus' actions and teaching which suggest a wider outlook than a merely Jewish one are emphasised. Luke records the healing of the centurion's servant (from Q) and also the healing and the gratitude of the Samaritan leper (from L). The teaching in the parables of the Prodigal Son and the Good Samaritan would appeal to Gentile readers.

(ii) Romans are presented here as favourable to Jesus, or at least as not hostile. Luke says that three times Pilate attempted to release Jesus, having acquitted him (23: 4, 14, 20, 22) and the blame for the crucifixion is put on the Jews (23: 25; 24: 20). There is the same note in the Acts, where stress is laid on the neutral attitude of Roman officials like Gallio (Acts 18: 12ff).

(iii) The story is put in a world-setting. Reference is made to the reigning Emperor at the time of Jesus' birth (2: 1) and the beginning of John's (and presumably Jesus') preaching (3: 1).

LUKE'S PORTRAIT OF JESUS

These aspects of the life and teaching of Jesus are found in this Gospel:

(i) His attitude towards the poor and outcast. Jesus blesses the poor (6: 20-21; cf. Matt. 5: 3, 6). In three parables the dangers of wealth are pointed out (12: 14ff; 16: 1ff, 19ff). Jesus befriends a sinful woman (7: 37ff), a crucified criminal (23: 39-43), tax-collectors and sinners (15: 1ff; 19: 1-10).

(ii) Women are mentioned with special tenderness and interest. Mary and Elizabeth are the central figures in the first two chapters. Jesus has sympathy for a widow (7: 12) and for both Mary and Martha (10: 38-42) and the weeping women of Jerusalem (23: 27ff). Not only men but women figure in the Lukan parables (15: 3-7, 8-10).

(iii) Samaritans and Gentiles are treated differently from the other Gospels. From the beginning Jesus' mission cannot be confined to the Jews (4: 24ff). He refuses to avenge himself on a Samaritan village (9: 52–56) and makes one of that despised race the hero of a parable (10: 30–35) and an incident (17: 12ff).

(iv) Luke mentions the Spirit of God more than any other evangelist. This is central in the birth stories (1: 15, 35, 67; 2: 25–26). Jesus is guided by the Spirit (4: 1, 14, 18; 10: 21) and the highest gift to men from God is his Spirit (11: 13; cf. Matt. 7: 11, which probably represents the wording in Q).

(v) Prayer is prominent in Luke's Gospel. He gives instances of Jesus' praying — at his baptism (3: 21), before choosing the disciples (6: 12), at Caesarea Philippi (9: 18), before teaching about prayer (11: 1ff) and on the cross (23: 34, 46). Three parables about prayer are found only in Luke (11: 5–9; 18: 1–8, 9–14). Hymns of praise are found at the beginning of the story (1: 46ff, 67ff; 2: 14, 29ff) and the book ends on the same note (24: 52–53).

The Authorship of the Book

The conclusion drawn from the opening phrases in Luke and the Acts is confirmed by other considerations. The Greek style is the same in both books and there are the same general ideas and 'scheme'. In the Gospel Luke traces the story of Jesus from Galilee to Jerusalem; in the Acts he traces the spread of Christianity from Jerusalem to Rome. The following are the main reasons for attaching the name of Luke to both these books:

(i) Early tradition and testimony is that the author was named Luke. As he was a comparatively obscure member of the Church, it is difficult to imagine their

THE GOSPEL OF LUKE

being attributed to him unless he had at least some hand in their composition.

(ii) In the Acts there are three sections, known as the 'we-passages', where the writer uses the first person plural instead of the third person (16: 10-17; 20: 6 to 21: 18; 28: 1-16). The obvious conclusion is that the writer was himself present on these occasions and he seems to be reproducing matter from a diary. Our investigation is thus narrowed to finding among Paul's circle of companions one who was present with him.

(iii) There are phrases in the books which suggest a medical knowledge — 'a great fever' (Luke 4: 38), 'full of leprosy' (in the advanced stages) (5: 12), 'his feet and ankle-bones received strength' (Acts 3: 7). The somewhat unkind words of Mark about doctors (5: 26) are modified in Luke (8: 43). But Cadbury subjected the language of the two books to a thorough examination and concluded that it is not more technical than might be expected from an educated layman of the first century. This does not, of course, rule out the possibility that the writer was a doctor, but it does not prove he was; the question cannot be decided on the ground of the language alone.

(iv) When we study the names of Paul's companions in the Acts and his own letters, some are naturally excluded — for instance Silas and Timothy, who are mentioned by name in the Acts, the former in a 'we-passage' (16: 19ff). Among those who are left, the most likely is Luke, whom Paul refers to in affectionate terms, as a doctor, in Colossians 4: 14.

It seems therefore that Luke had at least something to do with the writing of these books. There are two possibilities:

(i) Luke, the companion and friend of Paul, wrote

all of both books. In the Acts he included extracts from his own diary. He may have gathered some of the material for the Gospel when living at Caesarea during Paul's two years of imprisonment there. There are traits in the Gospel which remind us of Paul's teaching; the apostle's doctrine of justification by faith can be found in the parable of the Prodigal Son, and his declaration that in Christ 'there can be neither Jew nor Greek, bond nor free, male nor female' (Gal. 3: 28) is also echoed in the Gospel.

(ii) Luke wrote only the diary, when he was with Paul on his journeys. Another writer made use of this as a source and incorporated it into his book. He rewrote it in his own style (retaining only 'we' in some places — for the diary may originally have extended over more than the three passages where this now appears), just as he did with Mark in the Gospel. Those who hold this view stress the differences between the narrative in the Acts and the information given by Paul himself in his letters, and the differences between the portraits of Paul in the two. Hence the author cannot have been the close companion of Paul that the diarist was. It was, of course, this author who also wrote the Gospel. The name of Luke became attached to the two books because he was the diarist.

The Date of Composition of Luke's Gospel

Three dates have been suggested for this:

(i) A very early one. The Acts ends with the imprisonment of Paul at Rome (28: 30–31) and some have felt that Luke would not have ended there if he had known of Paul's execution, which probably happened in A.D. 64–65. Hence the book (and the Gospel

THE GOSPEL OF LUKE

also) is to be dated before that. It has been suggested that they were written to 'brief' the counsel for Paul's defence at his trial.

There are great difficulties in the way of such an early date, however. Luke's language in 21: 20, where he interprets the vague reference in Mark 13: 14 as meaning the siege of Jerusalem, shows that he at least knew of the events of A.D. 69. Further, the early date would make Mark about A.D. 60 and we have seen that the probable date for Mark's Gospel itself is 65–70.

(ii) A very late date. Some think that Luke had read the *Antiquities of the Jews*, by Josephus (which was published about A.D. 96), for the Jewish historian mentions a Lysanias (cf. Luke 3: 1) who was put to death in 34 B.C. In this case Luke is wrong in his reference here. This would, however, ascribe great carelessness to Luke, if he took the name from Josephus' book and inserted it in this unsuitable place. An inscription has been discovered which suggests that a man called Lysanias ruled Abilene in the time of Tiberius.

The other suggested case of dependence on Josephus is Acts 5: 36–37, where Luke mentions Theudas and Judas, in the report of Gamaliel's advice. One difficulty is that he has put the two men in the wrong order — Judas revolted against the Romans in A.D. 6 and Theudas in A.D. 44; another puzzle is that Theudas' date is about ten years after Gamaliel's speech. Josephus mentions Theudas and then the sons of Judas, and it is suggested again that Luke carelessly read Josephus' words. But his reliance on the written account is not proved. Streeter suggested that Luke heard Josephus lecture in Rome, some years before the publication of his book, and remembered the two names from hearing them in this way. In any case, Luke was not directly concerned with Jewish history and it is pardonable if he confused the two men.

(iii) An intermediate date — between 75 and 85. The Gospel is probably later than the siege of Jerusalem (cf. Luke 21: 20). It is later than Mark (65–70) and time must be allowed for Mark to have become known, so that a copy was available for Luke. The Acts shows that the author probably did not know the contents of Paul's letters; his book was written before these were copied and came into general circulation. The reason why he finished his second book with the arrival of Paul at Rome and not with his trial and execution is that he reached his goal at this point. Paul had arrived at Rome; to have told the story of his fate at the hands of the Romans would have been an anti-climax. He may, of course, have intended the writing of a third volume.

If the Proto-Luke theory is accepted, the first draft of the Gospel would be earlier — perhaps on the arrival at Rome or between 60 and 64. The final edition of the book, combining Markan matter with Q and L material, would still be about A.D. 80. The Gospel was known to Clement of Rome (writing about 96) and probably to the writer of the Fourth Gospel (95–105), so the date is once again fixed before the last decade of the first century.

CHAPTER X

JESUS' TEACHING ABOUT MAN

THERE is little that is systematic in the accounts of Jesus' teaching in the Gospels. We have no record of any set discourse on any particular topic. Even the Sermon on the Mount, which is considered by some people to be the essence of Jesus' teaching, is really a collection of sayings on a number of subjects, arranged very skilfully by the author of Matthew. Most of this was probably delivered on a variety of occasions and the original setting has been lost. Much of Jesus' teaching seems indeed to have been given not in any formal way but as occasion demanded, in what may seem to us to be almost a haphazard fashion. This is, however, typical of the East. So we have to make a study of many separate passages in the Gospels in order to see what Jesus has to say on any particular topic.

It has been said that the teaching of Jesus may be classified under three headings — 'Myself', 'My brother' and 'God'. 'Myself' means his teaching about the individual; 'My brother' indicates what he had to say about men in their relations with each other — social teaching; 'God' means his message about God and the Kingdom of God. All three are of course intimately bound up with each other.

MYSELF'

Many peoples, ancient and recent, have had their thoughts about the ideal character. The Greeks enunciated four virtues which they considered the good man should exhibit — wisdom, self-control, righteousness and courage. Others have suggested that indifference to outward pains and pleasures alike was the mark of the ideal man. In more recent times, the 'super-man' has been held up as the goal of human effort. The difficulty that ordinary people have often felt about such teaching is that the ideal seems a long way beyond their reach. The Greek virtues were those of philosophers, a Stoical 'indifference' seems to be unattainable to most people who realise their human frailty, while the 'super-man' tends to despise the common folk. People require an ideal which can be or has been manifested in a human life, an example which they can really follow. One of the striking things about the portrait of Jesus in the Gospels is the way in which his own character harmonises with what he himself laid down for others.

Jesus' character was in one way a series of contrasts. People were constantly noticing his authority. The first remark of the people in the Capernaum synagogue was about the authority of his teaching (Mark 1: 22), which was repeated when his authority was shown in deeds as well (1: 27). The Roman centurion, himself a man of authority, acknowledged that Jesus had an even greater power (Luke 7: 7–8). Yet, along with his authority over men — friends and enemies alike — there was in Jesus a kindness which attracted little children to him (Mark 10: 13–16). He could be indignant against narrow-mindedness and hard-heartedness

(Mark 3: 5) and against entrenched wrong-doing in the Temple court (Mark 11: 15–16), yet he was tender towards the suffering and the sinful (Luke 7: 47–50 — a sinful woman; Luke 23: 39–43 — a crucified criminal). There is frequent mention of his compassion, both for individuals (Mark 1: 41) and for the crowds (Mark 6: 34), but he could also on occasion make stern demands on those whom he called to follow him (Luke 9: 57–62). Jesus was a social man, with a group of disciples, chosen 'that they might be with him' (Mark 3: 14) and his enemies named him 'the friend of tax-collectors and sinners' (Matt. 11: 19; Luke 7: 34); yet he sought solitude and relief from the crowds which thronged him (Mark 1: 35; 7: 24).

There is indeed in the character of Jesus a poise and balance which is seldom, if ever, achieved by other men. In spite of living a very busy life, so that twice Mark says that he could not even eat a meal (3: 20; 6: 31), he was not distracted and one never has the impression that things were being done in a hurry or a panic. He could rejoice over the triumph of his disciples and in fellowship with God (Luke 10: 21), yet could sorrow over the fate of Jerusalem (Luke 19: 41–44). Throughout his teaching there is alertness of mind and insight into first principles. He recognised the two commandments which sum up all the Jewish religious laws (Mark 12: 29–31), and he dealt with the Old Testament regulations, discriminating between the more permanent parts and those which had to be superseded by a new spirit, in a way which we today call the critical method (Matt. 5: 21–48).

One with such a character is indeed the person to whom one would go for teaching about the individual.

Jesus himself had much to do with individuals. In addition to his public teaching, there are recorded in the Gospels a number of interviews with individuals, when he was concerned with one particular man or woman. He spoke in three parables of the value of the individual, even if that was one in a hundred (Luke 15: 3–7 — the Lost Sheep), one in ten (15: 8–10 — the Lost Coin) or one of two (15: 11–32 — the Prodigal Son).

What Jesus has to say about 'Myself' may be summarised under four aspects.

(i) The Beatitudes (Matt. 5: 3–12; Luke 6: 20–23) show Jesus' view of the people who are really 'blessed' or 'happy'. (The Greek term may be translated by either word; they are the people who are to be congratulated or pronounced really happy.) They may not be the type whom the world counts happy, but they have the springs of true blessedness within them. Jesus is not here laying down a law which men must struggle to follow but painting a picture of men as they would be if they accepted the realm of God.

The highest ideal for man's conduct is elsewhere summarised as obedience to two commandments — love towards God and love towards one's neighbour (Mark 12: 29–31; Luke 10: 27–28). The Beatitudes show the character of the man in whose life these two principles are fundamental.

(ii) Jesus recognised also the imperfections in human nature. This is implied in his first preaching — a call to repent (Mark 1: 15). If men were already perfect there would be no need for repentance. Jesus was fully aware of the sins of men. The sinner was an offender against God. More than once Jesus used the metaphor of debt (Matt. 18: 23–35; Luke 7: 41–43). There was

JESUS' TEACHING ABOUT MAN

a debt which man himself could not pay, so God forgave him. Men, he realises, are 'lost' but they can be 'found' (Luke 15 — the sheep, the coin and the son who were lost and found; Luke 19: 10 — the tax-collector Zacchaeus). Jesus, however, constantly insists that God's forgiveness is dependent on men's forgiveness of those who have wronged them. If they do not forgive, God will not (which is the same thing as saying that he cannot) forgive them (Mark 11: 25; Matt. 6: 14-15; 18: 23-35).

It has been remarked by T. R. Glover that Jesus says little about 'sin', as a general term or an abstraction, but much about men's 'sins'. His teaching is that these are not so much a matter of outward action as of inward motive and state of mind. 'From within, out of the heart of men', proceed evil things (Mark 7: 21-22). This is the point of Jesus' comparisons between the law of the Old Testament and his teaching in the Sermon on the Mount. In five instances he quotes the old commandment ('Thou shalt not' is the beginning for three of them — Matt. 5: 21, 27, 33, 38, 43), but proceeds: 'but I say to you . . .' The old Law spoke of outward actions — killing, committing adultery, taking an oath, recompense for injuries. Jesus spoke of inward impulses — evil thoughts, anger, malice, the spirit of retaliation.

(iii) The quality which was most praised and insisted on by Jesus may be called 'genuineness'. He encouraged his disciples to possess the 'single eye' (Matt. 6: 22). This means singleness of purpose, clarity and steadfastness of intention. The person who has not the single eye is not sure what his principles are or what he is aiming at in life. His whole personality is 'full of darkness' (Matt. 6: 23). He is like the man who tries to serve two masters. 'You cannot be a slave to God and mammon (wealth)' (Matt. 6: 24). Sincerity, in thought, feeling and action, is what Jesus demands.

That is why he denounced the Pharisees; they were not bad men, full of evil actions; the trouble with them was that they were not genuine. They were playing a part, deceiving even themselves. The term he used of them was 'hypocrites' (Mark 7: 6; 12: 15; Matt. 6: 2, 5, 16; 23: 13) — a Greek word which originally meant an actor. In the Greek theatre actors wore masks and so did not have to display in their faces the emotions they were supposed to affect. The term came to be applied to anyone who played a part without really meaning or feeling it. In contrast to such men, Jesus asked of his followers sincerity in thought, feeling and action.

(iv) Throughout Jesus' teaching there is constant emphasis on practice. The members of his true family, he declares, are those who hear the word of God and do it (Mark 3: 35). Those who are accepted in the Kingdom of God are not those who utter lip-service but those who do the will of the Father (Matt. 7: 21). The Sermon on the Mount and the Sermon on the Plain both finish with the parable of the Two Foundations. Here the man whose house was well-founded, so that it stood the storms, was the one who not only listened to Jesus' teaching but practised it (Matt. 7: 24–27; Luke 6: 47–49).

Jesus' teaching about the individual is summarised in a phrase of his own — 'You therefore shall be perfect, as your heavenly Father is perfect' (Matt. 5: 48). This saying has given rise to much misunderstanding, some people considering it as an impossible ideal. The Greek term used and the context, however, help to explain what Jesus meant. The Greek word for 'perfect' (*teleios*) means 'fulfilling an end' (*telos*), a function. As God fulfils his function in the eternal sphere, so men must fulfil theirs, in their own world. The previous verses have spoken of mercy, forgiveness of one's enemies and love towards all. This is the way in which men can imitate God and so be 'perfect'. As God loves all, friends and enemies alike, and does them good, so men must treat each other.

In treating of Jesus' ideal for the individual, we have naturally gone on to his ideal for their relations with their fellows. So this section — 'Myself' — cannot be separated from the next — 'My brother'.

'My Brother'

The character of the individual must be worked out in society. No man lives to himself; he is always a member of some social group, small or large. Jesus counsels his disciples to remember that their words and actions influence other people and show what kind of people they themselves really are. Like lights in the world, they cannot be hidden; so they must illuminate men (Matt. 5: 14–16). Like salt, if they lose their savour they are worthless (Matt. 5: 13).

Jesus laid down no hard-and-fast rules for conduct and outlined no ideal social state. He dealt rather with principles which should govern all conduct. There are three in particular which should guide men in their social relations.

(i) *The breaking down of barriers*

There were barriers between men in the first-century world no less than in the twentieth — social, religious, political and racial. Jesus broke down the social barrier by inviting all men to be his disciples, irrespective of their class or occupation — poor people, labouring men like fishers in Galilee and the rich tax-collector of Jericho. Need was his only criterion. He disregarded the religious barrier by mixing not only with people who attended the synagogue but also with those who were considered outside the pale by the strict religious Jews (Mark 2: 13-16). He was scorned as a 'friend of tax-collectors and sinners' (Matt. 11: 19; Luke 7: 34). The political barrier was broken when he included among his chosen company such diverse characters as Matthew the tax-collector and Simon the Zealot (Matt. 10: 3-4).

The racial barrier was perhaps the greatest and the most difficult one to overcome. Jews hated especially the Samaritans, who returned their hatred with interest. Jesus' own disciples illustrated the conventional attitude when they asked Jesus to punish the churlish Samaritans who refused to allow Jesus and his company lodging for the night in their village (Luke 9: 54-56). Jesus, however, 'turned and rebuked them — and they went on to another village'. When Jesus wished to give an example of true neighbourliness, in answer to the lawyer's querulous query, 'Who is my neighbour?', he deliberately chose a Samaritan, after the Jewish priest and Levite had failed to do their brotherly duty (Luke 10: 30-35). When he healed ten lepers, one only came back to give thanks and received commendation from Jesus — 'and he was a Samaritan' (Luke 17: 16).

Even greater perhaps than the barrier between Jew and Samaritan was that between the Jew and the out-and-out foreigner, the Gentile. Although some of the Pharisees were keen to make proseltyes and there were some Gentiles, known as the 'God-fearers', who joined with Jews in worship in the synagogues, the attitude of most of the people of Palestine was that the Gentiles were 'dogs'. Here also Jesus' actions speak more loudly even than his words. There are at least two occasions in the Synoptic Gospels on which Jesus came into contact with Gentiles. A Roman centurion asked Jesus to heal his servant. Jesus was amazed at his confidence in him and declared that this faith exceeded anything he had found 'in Israel' (Luke 7: 9; Matt. 8: 10). When he visited the district of Tyre and Sidon, a Syro-Phoenician woman, a Greek, wished him to heal her daughter. Although Jesus seemed at first to adopt the usual scornful attitude of the Jews towards such people, he consented to attend to her request, pleased with the woman's ready reply (Mark 7: 24–30).

(ii) *Reconciliation between men and forgiveness*

This is the part which the individual can play in the breaking down of barriers. The human problem is that of reconciling to each other men who have become estranged. People — including the Jews of Jesus' day — had tried the way of retaliation towards those who hated them. Jesus suggests another way, that of forgiveness — non-resistance and loving one's enemies.

Matthew gives this teaching as part of Jesus' treatment of the old Law (Matt. 5: 38–42, 43–48). Luke reproduces it (probably from Q) in one passage, without any reference to the Old Testament (Luke 6: 27–35). Jesus takes here extreme instances of the way in which his new spirit of love and forgiveness might work out in life. We must bear in mind what has been said already about eastern exaggeration; men did not go about then smiting one another on the cheek without cause, any more than they do now, as a normal thing!

This is probably the most difficult and the most contested part of Jesus' teaching. The form of the sayings in Luke (6: 27-28) shows, however, what he meant by 'love'. This was active goodness towards one's enemies as well as one's friends. To love people did not mean to be sentimental about them but meant 'do them good' and wish them well. Jesus is counselling this method, as a way of reconciliation; at least it could not do more harm than the old way of retaliation!

This seems particularly to be applied to the enemies of the Jews at that time, the Romans. The phrase about 'going a second mile' (Matt. 5: 41) is a reference to the custom by which a soldier of the army of occupation could make a native carry his pack for a mile. Jesus suggests that the latter should offer to go another mile, in addition to the compulsory one.

The reason given by Jesus why men should adopt such conduct is noteworthy. It is not that they might thereby solve political, racial or social problems (although this result may follow), but that they might have the greatest reward of all — that of being like their Father (Matt. 5: 45-48; Luke 6: 35-36). Jesus says that God treats men like that; therefore they should treat each other in the same way.

Jesus himself is the greatest exemplar of this attitude. In spite of opposition he went on quietly with his work. From the time of his arrest in Gethsemane until his death on the cross, through the trials and mocking, he refused to 'answer back' or to denounce his enemies. At the end he prayed on the cross for their forgiveness (Luke 23: 34).

(iii) *Service*

Service of one's fellows, even to the point of sacrifice, is constantly urged by Jesus. He enforces this both by parable, by direct word and by example. In one of his most famous stories, Jesus pictures the judgment of the nations (Matt. 25: 31–46). He was probably making use of a picture of the Judgment by the Son of Man which had been written in an apocalyptic work, the Book of Enoch. The usual criterion among the Jews of acceptance or rejection by God was whether they had kept the Law faithfully or not. Jesus here dramatically changes the test; it is whether men have fed the hungry, clothed the naked, visited the sick and imprisoned — their service of their fellows (25: 34–36).

When James and John demanded the chief places in the coming 'glory' of the Messiah, Jesus told them that they were not to be like the rulers of the world but were to be 'servants' and 'slaves' (Mark 10: 35–45) — the literal meaning of the Greek words in 10: 43–44. According to Luke there arose even at the Last Supper a similar dispute about greatness, and Jesus enforced the same lesson there (Luke 22: 24–26) — that they must serve others instead of being served themselves.

The service which leads to sacrifice was expressed in a paradox — the one who saves his life loses it, while the one who loses his life saves it. This saying was probably frequently on the lips of Jesus. It is reported in Mark (8: 35 — cf. Matt. 16: 25 and Luke 9: 24) and was also included in Q, from which it is reproduced in Matthew 10: 39 and Luke 17: 33.

As in the rest of Jesus' teaching, his own practice is

the greatest example of this. After Peter had acknowledged him as Messiah at Caesarea Philippi, Jesus began to teach the disciples that the Son of Man must suffer (Mark 8: 31). The final sentence in the paragraph about the request of James and John runs: 'Even so — or also — the Son of Man came not to be served but to serve' (Mark 10: 45). At the Last Supper, after reminding the disciples that by the world's standard the man who sits at table is superior to the one who serves him, Jesus concluded: 'But I am in the midst of you as one who serves' (Luke 22: 27). Jesus' life was one of service, in which he gave himself without stint to all who were in need, healing and teaching and helping. His thoughts were not for himself but for others; even in the hours just before the betrayal by Judas he had time to think and pray for Peter (Luke 22: 32), and he went to his death with a word of pity for the women of Jerusalem (Luke 23: 28) and encouragement for the crucified criminal (Luke 23: 43).

(iv) *Teaching on specific topics*

It is not often that Jesus has something to say about particular social problems. It was his aim and purpose rather to give general counsel, to lay down principles which could be applied to differing circumstances, not to legislate for particular occasions. There were, however, some social and ethical matters on which Jesus had something more precise to say.

We may note, for instance, his attitude towards wealth and rich people. For some men, he realised, wealth was the great hindrance, so that 'it is easier for a camel to go through the eye of a needle than for a rich man to enter the Kingdom of God' (Mark 10: 25).

JESUS' TEACHING ABOUT MAN

Jesus said this after a rich man had come to him enquiring what he had to do to gain eternal life. He had kept the Law; but because there was one stumbling-block in his life still, Jesus told him to sell all and give to the poor, as a preliminary to following him (Mark 10: 17–22). The same thought is present in the story of Jesus' meeting with Zacchaeus, the rich tax-collector of Jericho (Luke 19: 1–10). Zacchaeus himself realised this and made a generous offer — to give half of his goods to the poor and to restore four-fold what he had taken wrongfully. Jesus welcomed this gesture and praised the man (19: 9).

Jesus himself, however, numbered rich people among his friends and followers. The tax-collector Levi was possibly a rich man (Mark 2: 14); Zacchaeus certainly was (Luke 19: 2). Joseph of Arimathaea is spoken of in Matthew as 'a rich man' (Matt. 27: 57). (Mark's phrase, 'a councillor of honourable estate' (15: 43), may imply the same.) The man who provided the room for the Last Supper had a house with 'a large upper room' — big enough for a number of men to have a meal together (Mark 14: 15). Luke says that some women in Galilee, who evidently had a considerable income, 'ministered to him of their substance' (Luke 8: 3) — that is, they helped him out of their own resources.

Far indeed from condemning wealth and its possession in general, Jesus urged the responsibility of those who had it. This is the emphasis in the parable of the rich man and the beggar Lazarus (Luke 16: 19–31). The importance of the parable is not in the references to conditions after death. Jesus was here making use of current Jewish ideas and terms. The teaching he wished to convey is the responsibility of those who were rich and the hardening effect of wealth on men. A similar lesson can be discerned in the parable of the Talents (Matt. 25: 14–30) and that of the Pounds (Luke 19: 12–27); these may be variants of the same story. Although their primary reference is to the Kingdom of God, we may also see depicted the right human attitude towards the responsibilities of life.

Jesus deprecated trust in wealth, for such tended to make man its slave. The trouble with the rich foolish man was not that he decided to build greater barns in which to store his produce — this was only reasonable business policy — but that he then thought that he was quite secure, with 'much goods laid up for many years', and could 'eat, drink and be merry', with nothing else to worry about and nothing deeper in life to consider (Luke 12: 16–21). 'Where your treasure is, there will your heart be also.' Man cannot be a slave to God and wealth (Luke 12: 34; 16: 13; Matt. 6: 21, 24). A man might gain the whole world of material things and lose the most important part — his own life or soul (Mark 8: 36).

Jesus' attitude towards another topic of burning importance — politics and the State — is not often referred to in the Gospels. On one occasion the Pharisees joined with the Herodians, in order to trap him, and asked whether the Jews ought to pay their taxes to the Roman authorities or not (Mark 12: 13–17). By possessing coins with the image of Caesar on them, the Jews were acknowledging the Romans as their overlords. Jesus then pointed out that, as they were indebted to the State, they should do something to repay the debt — 'render (give back) to Caesar what is his'. But he also laid down a principle of far-reaching application — that there are certain things over which

JESUS' TEACHING ABOUT MAN

the State has no claim — 'the things that are God's'. He did not define the exact extent of the claims of Caesar and the claims of God. That was left for the sincere enquirer to think out for himself.

With prophetic insight Jesus saw into the political situation of the Jews in his time no less than into their moral and religious condition. There is a warning to them in Luke 13: 1–5. Jesus was told of the disaster which befell Jews who were resisting the Romans — Galilaeans plotting to rise against Pilate and eighteen men who were apparently undermining a tower-fortification. Jesus said that unless the Jews repented of their way of life, their violence and dreams of rebellion, they would all similarly perish. He reinforced this warning by the parable of the unfruitful fig-tree (Luke 13: 6–9). He foresaw the siege and destruction of Jerusalem by the Romans and wept to realise what it would mean (Luke 19: 41–44).

Jesus set forth no details of a particular social or political system which men ought to establish. If he had done so, his teaching would have become outmoded. Instead he laid down the basic principles of a society in which God could reign, where barriers would be broken down, where men would be reconciled to each other and where men would serve one another even as he himself had served them.

The teaching of Jesus about 'My brother' is well summed-up in the Golden Rule — Treat men as you would have them treat you (Luke 6: 31; Matt. 7: 12), and indeed as God treats them and you. If men realised God as their Father, they would acknowledge other men as their brothers. If they realised men as their brothers, they would act towards them as such. If they were forgiving towards their enemies, they would be acting as God himself acts (Matt. 5: 45; Luke 6: 35).

So we see that whereas 'Myself' leads to 'My brother', both of these really depend on the third aspect of Jesus' teaching — 'God'.

CHAPTER XI

'GOD AND HIS MESSIAH'

Jesus' first proclamation in Galilee is summarised by Mark as 'good news of God' (Mark 1: 14).

The Jews had many words which they used for God. In Old Testament days the God of the Hebrews was known by a name which consisted of four Hebrew consonants, YHWH, which was probably pronounced Yahweh. It is represented in English translations generally as THE LORD, sometimes by the common misspelling Jehovah. Because of their reverence even for the 'name' of God, the Jews ceased to pronounce the sacred word and when they came across it in reading they substituted 'The Lord' for it. In Jesus' time they frequently referred to God in this way. There were other titles for him also. After the return from Exile they had tended to stress the transcendence of God. One consequence of this was that they preferred not to speak of him directly but by periphrases such as 'the Power', 'the Almighty', 'the King', 'the Heaven' or 'the Blessed'. So the writer of Matthew's Gospel, out of deference to Jewish prejudice, substituted the term Kingdom of Heaven for Mark's Kingdom of God.

Jesus' Teaching About God

We find in the Gospels that Jesus seldom used such phrases. He spoke directly of God. The name which he particularly used for God was not one which emphasised his transcendence but the simple one of 'Father'. This also would not be a completely new thought to his contemporaries. Writers in the Old Testament had thought of God as Father, especially as the Father of Israel the nation (Deut. 32: 6; Isa. 63: 16; Mal. 2: 10). Israel was consequently his son and in Hosea there is a striking picture of the father trying to teach his infant son to walk (Hos. 11: 3). God acts as a father who loves and pities his children (Ps. 103: 13). The Jewish Rabbis also sometimes stressed the fatherhood of God. They addressed God in prayer as 'Father' or as 'Father in heaven'.

Hence Jesus was not enunciating completely new teaching when he spoke of God as Father. The significant point is that this was Jesus' almost constant word for God and that in his teaching the conception became central.

The following is a list of places in the Synoptic Gospels where Jesus speaks of God as Father. (This is adapted from T. W. Manson's *The Teaching of Jesus*, pp. 94-98). There are four occurrences in Mark — 8: 38; 11: 25; 13: 32; 14: 36. Passages from Q contain the name eight or nine times — found in Luke 6: 36; 10: 21, 22; 11: 13; 12: 30, 32, and in Matthew (where this Gospel has 'Father' for another phrase in Luke) 5: 45; 10: 20, 29, 32, 33; 6: 26; 7: 21. Passages found only in Matthew have it about twenty-three times: Matthew 5: 16; 6: 4, 6, 8, 9, 14, 15, 18; 13: 43; 15: 13; 16: 17; 17: 10; 18: 14, 19, 35; 23: 9; 25: 34; 26: 42, 53; 28: 19. Passages found only in Luke have it six times: Luke 2: 49; 11: 2; 22: 29; 23: 34; 23: 46; 24: 49.

Examination of these passages has shown that Jesus

'GOD AND HIS MESSIAH'

used the term mainly when speaking to the disciples or when in prayer. The Fatherhood of God was first indeed part of his own experience of God. At his baptism he had known the presence of the Spirit of God and had realised that God was saying to him: 'Thou art my beloved Son' (Mark 1: 11). Thenceforward he knew God as his own Father. It was because of this knowledge that he could declare that 'all things had been delivered' to him, so that he knew the Father and the Father knew him (Matt. 11: 27; Luke 10: 22). As at the beginning of his ministry, so at the end Jesus was conscious of God as his Father. In Gethsemane he prayed 'Abba — Father' (Mark 14: 35-36), using the Aramaic term which he had probably first learned from his own mother, and even on the cross the name was twice on his lips (Luke 23: 34, 46).

Jesus would make this consciousness of God as Father part of the experience of all men. They should think of God in this way in their prayers; they were to begin with 'Father' (Luke 11: 2). (To this short form of prayer, found in Luke 11: 2-4, as given in the R.V., the author of Matthew has added typical Jewish phrases — Matt. 6: 9-15.) Men may ask confidently for good things because God is at least as ready to give as men are willing to give to their own children (Matt. 7: 11; Luke 11: 13). Men are urged not to worry — not for any prudential reason but simply because God is their Father and knows their wants (Luke 12: 30; Matt. 8: 32). Finally, the individual counts because God is his Father and cares for him. The name of God is not actually mentioned in the parable of the Prodigal Son (Luke 15: 11-32), but we are surely justified in seeing in the father of the boy a picture of God, desiring to receive the wanderer home again and anxious over his solitary lost son, as the shepherd was anxious over his lost sheep and the woman over her one coin (Luke 15: 7, 10).

When men realise this and respond they become God's children. To be called 'sons of God' is the highest ideal for men (Matt. 5: 9, 45; cf. Luke 6: 35). In the Semitic idiom the term indicated one who partook of the character of God, just as a 'son of truth' meant a truthful man, a 'son of peace' a peace-loving man, a 'son of the devil' an evil man. It is as true of Jesus' teaching as it is of Paul's, about which it has been remarked that 'God is the Father of all men but not all men are his sons'.[1]

The God of Jesus was thus no abstract conception, a philosophical theory. He was a God of intimate relations with men. He was a God of action, not of passive inactivity. This thought also is rooted in the Old Testament. Yahweh was the 'God who speaks' and does things. He spoke and acted through kings and through prophets. When the prophets said that the 'word of Yahweh came' to them, they used a term (*dabar*) which meant both word and deed. Towards the close of the Old Testament period and in the time of Jesus it was particularly expected that God would speak and act through the Messiah.

The Jewish Messianic Idea

The term Messiah means literally 'anointed'. In the Old Testament the adjective was applied to kings — the usual term for a Hebrew king was 'the Lord's

[1] C. Ryder Smith: *The Bible Doctrine of Man*, p. 212.

'GOD AND HIS MESSIAH'

anointed' — and to prophets (1 Kings 19: 6; Isa. 61: 1). Even a foreign king, Cyrus the Persian, is called the 'anointed' of Yahweh by Deutero-Isaiah (Isa. 45: 1). But the term Messiah is never applied in the Old Testament to a *future* king.

The idea of a 'Messianic hope' in the Old Testament takes a variety of forms. There was first the general expectation of a time of righteousness and prosperity in the future, in contrast to the present bad times. This would be established by God himself. The prophets and others spoke of this often in quite general terms. Then some passages speak of a righteous kingdom, wherein God's faithful worshippers would be vindicated and his will would be done. From this it was but natural to think of a righteous king, who would reign in the future. So an earthly ruler was spoken of, who would act as God's vicegerent. He was generally thought of as belonging to the royal line of David. When, however, this line ceased, with the capture of Jerusalem in 586 B.C., the future king was considered as an idealised David. He was to conquer his enemies and would then rule righteously, by his might. His kingdom was often thought of as a universal one. There is no suggestion that he was regarded as otherwise than human and mortal. In the Old Testament he is never actually called the Messiah; but it was from this seed that the later application grew.[1]

In the apocalpytic works, both in the Old Testament and in the period between the Testaments, the idea of a future king became more clearly defined. Only once is there any suggestion that the king would come

---

[1] For illustrations of all these points, see the valuable chapter on 'The Hebrew Messiah' in C. Ryder Smith's *Bible Doctrine of Salvation*.

not as a warrior but in peace (Zech. 9: 9–10). The apocalyptic writers thought that God would intervene in the midst of calamity and tragedy and establish his righteous Kingdom. After the close of the Old Testament the future king comes definitely to be called the Messiah. There appeared also the figure of the Son of Man, who would come in glory.

By the time of Jesus there was a general expectation among the Jews of a universal reign of God. Many Old Testament passages were regarded as Messianic which had not originally this meaning at all. Thus Psalm 2, which referred to a reigning king to whom God gave his authority, so that he was called his son (2: 7ff), was taken to indicate the Messiah. In the mind of the people the hope of political freedom was associated with this expectation. The Messiah, the descendant of David, would restore the monarchy to Israel. A common idea was that the Messiah would appear in the wilderness, gather his followers and lead them to Palestine. His expected reign would be a vindication of the Jews; this was sometimes interpreted in narrow nationalistic terms. To use phrases from Luke's Gospel, it was to be 'redemption' for Israel, 'salvation from our enemies', 'the consolation of Israel' and 'the redemption of Jerusalem'. But wider ideas prevailed also, at least in some circles. Men would be 'guided into the way of peace'; there was to be 'a light for revelation for the Gentiles', as well as national illumination and deliverance.

The Pharisees were among those who believed in a Messiah, but the Rabbis mainly looked upon these and similar hopes with suspicion and scorn. Their chief concern was with the keeping of the Law. The people must prepare themselves for God's deliverance by

'GOD AND HIS MESSIAH'

faithfulness to the Law, as the expression of the will of God. Then the Kingdom of God would come.

We can see from some passages in the Gospels what some of the popular expectations at the time were like — Luke 1: 68–79; 2: 11, 25, 30–32, 38; Mark 1: 7–8; 10: 47; 14: 61; Matthew 12: 38; Luke 17: 20; 24: 21; John 4: 25; 7: 27, 31. Cf. Acts 1: 6.

JESUS AND THE MESSIAH

Into that situation Jesus came. In some ways he fulfilled these expectations but in many ways he did not. We can see how he altered the common conceptions of the Messiah by noticing his use of four terms which occur in the Gospels.

(i) *The Messiah* or the Christ (the Hebrew and Greek words respectively for 'the anointed') is a comparatively rare term in the Gospels. In Mark it is applied to Jesus only five times and it is not found in any Q passage in Luke or Matthew. It seems clear from the Synoptics that Jesus did not publicly proclaim himself as the Messiah. He left men to discover this for themselves.

Jesus probably became conscious of his Messiahship at his baptism by John. The 'voice' which spoke to him (Mark 1: 11) quoted from Psalm 2: 7: 'Thou art my son'. This Psalm, as mentioned above, was interpreted messianically in the first century. This realisation on the part of Jesus shows also the meaning of the narrative of the Temptation (Matt. 4: 1–11; Luke 4: 1–13). Jesus was faced with the popular ideas and the current expectations about the Messiah and had to decide whether he was going to take this way or not. He there rejected the ways of bribery (feeding the hungry people of Palestine with bread), of magical power and marvels (such as leaping from the Temple into the courts below) and of force (the way in which evil conquers in the world).

The first acknowledgment of Jesus as Messiah was made by Peter at Caesarea Philippi (Mark 8: 27ff). Jesus immediately began to show his disciples what he meant by Messiahship — not conquest and victory but service and suffering, even death. This idea of a suffering Messiah is not the conception found in the Old Testament or in contemporary Judaism.

There are other hints in the Gospels that Jesus regarded himself as the Messiah. When John the Baptist, in prison, sent messengers to him to ask whether he was the 'coming one', Jesus returned an indirect reply (Matt. 11: 4-5; Luke 7: 21-22), referring to his works and his preaching. There is here no direct claim to be Messiah, but there is the suggestion that, for those who could discern, the work of Jesus was messianic activity. The first time that Jesus was publicly hailed as Messiah was on his arrival at Jericho, when Bartimaeus, the blind beggar, called out: 'Son of David, have mercy on me' (Mark 10: 47). Jesus did not disclaim the title here either. The acclamation of the people at Jesus' entry into Jerusalem (Mark 11: 9-10) may have been messianic, but no public action to follow this up was taken by Jesus.

The first time Jesus claimed this dignity was at his trial, in answer to the question of the High Priest: 'Art thou the Christ, the son of the Blessed?' (Mark 14: 61-62). Jesus' reply is, however, variously reported. Mark has: 'I am' (although some manuscripts read: 'Thou sayest that I am'). Luke has: 'Ye say that I am' (22: 70), and Matthew: 'Thou hast said' (26: 64).

It appears that Jesus did not deny that he was the Messiah, although he could not accept the interpretation of the term which his contemporaries and enemies gave it. When he was brought before Pilate, one of the accusations made against him was that he claimed to be 'Christ, a king' (Luke 23: 2). His Jewish accusers would no doubt expect Pilate to understand this in a political sense.

From the Synoptic Gospels it thus appears that Jesus avoided the term Messiah, although he knew himself to be the Christ. He realised the misunderstanding and the dangers of a popular movement among the excitable people if he openly made a claim to fulfil the messianic expectations. It was left to his disciples, after the crucifixion and resurrection, to proclaim him openly as 'Lord and Messiah' (Acts 2: 36).

(ii) *The Son of Man* was the term which was most frequently used by Jesus. The origin of the phrase and its use in the Gospels are discussed in the next chapter. It is sufficient to say here that it was, in some quarters at any rate, apparently used as a designation for the Messiah. It was perhaps not open to the popular misunderstanding which endangered the use of the term Messiah. It will be seen below that Jesus combined with the name Son of Man the thought not of a supernatural conquering hero, as was the common conception, but of a suffering Servant.

(iii) *Son of God* comes also in the Gospels. It was applied in the Old Testament to kings and others, in the sense in which it has been described above (see p. 154). In the first century it was used particularly of the Messiah. The idea of Jesus as the Son of God appears sparingly in Mark and Q. It is the author of Matthew who introduces it most frequently, for he reports Jesus as speaking of 'My Father' in places where the other writers simply say 'God'.

There are two outstanding passages in the Synoptic Gospels where Jesus is spoken of as 'the Son'. One is the account of the baptism where Psalm 2: 7 was quoted (Mark 1: 11). This evidently was a noteworthy experience for Jesus. He realised the presence of the Spirit of God and felt a call to action and to service. The other passage is in Matthew 11: 25-27 and Luke 10: 21-22 — probably taken from Q. In this there is a prayer of thanksgiving, that God has 'hidden these things from the wise and understanding' and revealed them to the simple ('babes'). Jesus goes on to say that 'all things have been delivered' by the Father to the one who knows him, that is the Son. There is intimate knowledge of the Father by the Son and of the Son by the Father. Others may be brought into a similar relationship with God, through the Son who has first attained it. To them 'the Son will reveal him'.

The actual occasion of this utterance is not certain. In Matthew it follows the denunciation of the cities of Galilee, whereas in Luke it comes after the return of the seventy disciples and the rejoicing of Jesus over their work. This seems more natural than the situation in Matthew. It has, however, been suggested that the true occasion was at Caesarea Philippi. Whenever it was spoken, this declaration of knowledge of the Father is an expression of the religious experience of Jesus himself. Knowledge of God comes from fellowship with him. It is a revelation of the character and nature of God as he appeared to Jesus in a moment of spiritual insight. It is also a revelation of the work which God had set him to do.

In other places in the Synoptic Gospels the term Son of God obviously means the Messiah — Matthew 4: 3 (Luke 4: 3); Matthew 16: 16 (cf. Mark 8: 29); Mark 14: 61; Matthew 27: 40–43.

(iv) *The Servant* of God seems to have been a conception which was constantly in the mind of Jesus, even though the term may be sparsely used. The voice at the baptism spoke not only words from Psalm 2: 7 ('Thou art my beloved son') but continued: 'in thee I am well pleased'. This comes from Isaiah 42: 1: 'Behold my servant . . . in whom my soul delighteth.' This passage is from one of the five Servant Songs found in Deutero-Isaiah, wherein the poet is thinking of one who serves and suffers on behalf of men. The servant — one who was chosen from birth — had the spirit of God upon him. He had a mission to the nations, in the fulfilment of which he met with ostracism, suffering and even death. Nevertheless he was gentle, meek and nonresistant, thus carrying out God's purpose of love. It is still uncertain whether these poems refer to an individual or to the nation of Israel; they constitute at any rate an ideal for the nation, or the righteous people within the nation. The Jews of Jesus' day did not interpret them as referring to the Messiah. There was no thought of a Messiah who would act and suffer in this way.

The narrative of the baptism thus suggests that Jesus' experience here was not only that of being the Messiah but also of fulfilling the role of the Servant. There are other hints to the same effect in the Gospels. The words in Mark 10: 45 — 'the Son of Man came . . . to give his life a ransom for many' — probably reflect Isaiah 53: 11, where the Servant's sacrifice of himself is said to be for the benefit of 'many'. There is also an explicit reference in Luke 22: 37, where at the Last Supper Jesus quotes from Isaiah 53: 12 ('He was numbered with the transgressors'), as relating to himself. When he spoke in the synagogue service at Nazareth, he read from Isaiah 61: 1 — 'The spirit of the Lord is upon me . . .' This is not from one of the Servant Songs but it comes from a section which is akin to these poems in spirit and thought.

It seems that Jesus combined with the thought of the suffering Servant the term Son of Man, to denote his new conception of Messiahship. When he spoke of the Son of Man as suffering, being rejected by the leaders of the nation and being killed, he was departing from the popular conceptions both of the Messiah and the Son of Man. He was thinking of the Servant. This same combination is behind Mark 10: 45. After the Transfiguration he asked the disciples how it was 'written of the Son of Man, that he should suffer many things and be set at nought' (Mark 9: 12). But it was *not* written that the Son of Man would be treated in this way. It was, however, written of the Servant of God, in Isaiah 53, and it was this ideal which inspired Jesus.

The important question is thus not so much whether Jesus thought of himself as the Messiah as of what sort of Messiah. We may safely conclude that he was the Christ, but not the figure depicted in the Old Testament or the deliverer of popular expectation. God was at work, as the old writers had hoped, but in a different way from that which they had anticipated. He was at work through the words and deeds of one who was not only Messiah and Son of God but was also Servant and Son of Man.

In the latter part of this chapter we have been

considering the person of Jesus himself and the work which he felt he had come to do. This is intimately related with the topic with which we began — Jesus' teaching about God. Jesus did not deal theoretically with the character of God or speculate about his nature. He showed men God in action, in his own life and mission. God was Father and he was the one who sent the Messiah and who commissioned his Servant. He was also King, who was to establish his reign over the hearts and lives of men. To this aspect of Jesus' teaching we must now turn.

CHAPTER XII

THE KINGDOM OF GOD AND THE SON OF MAN

THE Kingdom of God was a phrase which was constantly on the lips of Jesus. It was indeed the central theme of his preaching and teaching. Mark states that his announcement in Galilee, at the beginning of his work, was 'The kingdom of God is at hand' (Mark 1: 15). This was the 'good news of God' which he had come to proclaim.

The term would not be a new one to his hearers. The phrase does not actually occur in the Old Testament, but there is continually expressed the thought of God as king. He was first of all king over the nation of Israel. Eventually the Jews came to see him as king over the world. In some ways the Kingdom of God — a better translation would be the Reign or kingly Rule of God[1] — was thought of as a present fact; but it was also a hope for the future, when God would really rule over men. Some thought of the Kingdom as earthly. Jerusalem was pictured as the centre of the new age. But others despaired of this present world and transferred the Kingdom to a coming age, which would be inaugurated by a resurrection of the dead and a judgment. In the time of Jesus the main thought of the Kingdom was of a glorious future

[1] Moffatt translates it throughout as 'the Realm' (occasionally 'Reign') of God.

state. The most familiar conception among the Jews was that the Kingdom would be won by and based on force, by the action of God himself. The Kingdom was to be for the Jews, the Gentiles being excluded. Some, however, held out a hope for good men of other nations as well. The chief emphasis was that it was to be *God's* Kingdom — a theocracy.

Jesus' teaching on the Kingdom of God

In his teaching Jesus spoke of the Kingdom in three main ways.

(i) Sometimes he suggested — and indeed definitely stated — that the Kingdom was actually present among men. On one occasion at least his opponents charged him with using the power of the 'prince of demons' to effect his cures. We have seen above (p. 39) how he answered this accusation. He went on to suggest an alternative explanation of his power. 'If I by the finger (or spirit) of God cast out demons, then the Kingdom of God has come upon you' (Luke 11: 20; Matt. 12: 28). The Kingdom had arrived, and its presence was shown in the work which Jesus was doing. A similar definite statement appears in Luke 17: 20–21. The expectations of men who sought for 'signs' of the coming of the Kingdom are set aside. The Kingdom of God does not come 'with observation' — 'as you hope to catch sight of it', as Moffatt translates. It is 'within you', or 'in the midst of you'. The exact translation is uncertain. If it is 'within you', Jesus was proclaiming the inward spiritual nature of the Kingdom, as opposed to the outward Kingdom of popular expectation. If it means 'among you', he was stating the actual presence of the Kingdom, as opposed to the conception of a future Reign. In either case the

Kingdom is thought of as a present reality. The Reign of God is here.

In other places the present tense is used when Jesus speaks of the Kingdom. From the time of John the Baptist, he says, men enter the Kingdom 'violently' (Luke 16: 16) or 'take it by force' (Matt. 11: 12). At another time he speaks of the humble man who 'is greatest in the Kingdom of Heaven' (Matt. 18: 4); again it is the present tense. To his disciples Jesus says the 'secret of the Kingdom' is now given (Mark 4: 11–12). The Kingdom already belongs to the poor (Luke 6: 20) — or the 'poor in spirit' (Matt. 5: 3) — and to the persecuted (Matt. 5: 10). It is for those who are like children (Mark 10: 14). It is God's will that it should be given to the disciples (Luke 12: 32). The scribe in Jerusalem is declared to be 'not far from the Kingdom of God' (Mark 12: 34). Despised folk and sinners 'go into the Kingdom of God' before the Pharisees (Matt. 21: 31).

Apart from these more definite statements, there are passages in the Gospels where Jesus seems to be thinking of the Kingdom as present, although it is not actually mentioned. In the synagogue at Nazareth he declared that 'the acceptable year of the Lord' had come, reading from Isaiah 61 (Luke 4: 18–21), which had been there 'fulfilled' in their ears. This would mean for his hearers the establishment of the Kingdom. In his answer to the messengers of John the Baptist from prison, Jesus referred to the works of his which they could witness (Luke 7: 22; Matt. 11: 4). The fact 'the blind receive their sight . . . and the poor have good news preached to them' was not only a hint that the Messiah had come but also suggested the presence of God's Kingdom in the midst of men, with its gracious results. Later Jesus declared that the disciples were blessed because they saw and heard certain things (Luke 10: 23f; cf. Matt. 13: 16f). By this he may have meant the Kingdom of God, now an actuality. In another connection Jesus said that 'something (the word is neuter) greater than Solomon is here'; this also may be a reference to God's reign (Matt. 12: 42; Luke 11: 31).

This aspect of Jesus' teaching has been emphasised by a school of interpretation which in recent years has become known as that of 'Realised Eschatology'. C. H. Dodd holds that the teaching of Jesus was intended to awake men to the reality of the presence of the Kingdom of God. It is held that the passages wherein Jesus speaks of the Kingdom as present are those which contain the really original thing about his message. The parables are interpreted along similar lines. The parables about growth — the Seed Growing (Mark 4: 26–29), the Mustard Seed (Matt. 13: 31f; Luke 13: 18f; cf. Mark 4: 30–32), the Leaven (Matt. 13: 33; Luke 13: 20f) — have their point in the climax of the story: the seed grows and produces a harvest, the mustard seed becomes a plant, the leaven makes the meal rise. These things were happening among men in Jesus' own ministry; the harvest was being reaped and the Kingdom had appeared. Other parables, such as that of the Ten Virgins (Matt. 25: 1–13), are interpreted along similar lines. They are warnings to the Jews, a comment on the unpreparedness of Judaism when the Messiah did come. They do not relate to a future crisis, as they are commonly interpreted, but to a situation which was already existent.

(ii) In other places Jesus plainly seems to consider the Kingdom of God as something for the future. It is a state of blessedness when God's rule will be acknowledged throughout the world. His first proclamation was: 'The Kingdom of God is at hand' (Mark 1: 15; Matt. 4: 17). This may mean simply 'within grasp', but it is still in the future. Later in his ministry, after the incident at Caesarea Philippi, Jesus declared that some of the bystanders among the disciples would not 'taste death until they see the Kingdom of God come with power' (Mark 9: 1). Various interpretations have been given of this passage. It evidently puzzled the other two Synoptic writers. Luke simply omitted the words 'come with power' (Luke 9: 27) and so made it a reference to the Kingdom within men's hearts. The writer of Matthew thought it referred to the coming of the Son of Man in his glory (Matt. 16: 28). The saying has been regarded in various other ways. It has been applied to the Transfiguration, which took place eight days later (Mark 9: 2ff), to the events of Pentecost, to the growth of the Church in the first century and even to the destruction of Jerusalem in A.D. 70. But the early Church regarded none of these as the coming of God's Kingdom and they do not fit in with Jesus' idea. If this saying is a genuine word of Jesus,[1] the Kingdom certainly seems to be thought of as future, even if in the near future, within that generation. But C. H. Dodd translates Mark 9: 1 as: '. . . until they have seen that the Kingdom of God has come with power'. It had already arrived and the disciples would realise this before long.

Jesus taught his followers to pray: 'Thy Kingdom come' (Luke 11: 2; Matt. 6: 10). They were thus to

---

[1] It is possible that the saying was originally the addition of a Christian preacher, who was assuring his hearers of the coming of the Kingdom within their own time.

look for a future consummation. He anticipated a time when men would come and 'sit down in the Kingdom' (Luke 13: 28f; Matt. 8: 11f). He told the disciples at the Last Supper that he would not drink wine until he 'drank it new in the Kingdom of God' (Mark 14: 25; Matt. 26: 29), while Luke says that he declared that he would not eat the Passover until it was 'fulfilled in the Kingdom of God' (Luke 22: 16).

The parables of the Tares (Matt. 13: 24-30) and the Drag-net (Matt. 13: 47-48) seem to refer to a future crisis or judgment and there are explanations attached to them in which the coming of the Kingdom is expressly identified with the day of Judgment and the 'consummation of the age' (translated incorrectly as 'the end of the world') (Matt. 13: 37-43, 49-50). It is, however, generally considered today that these interpretations do not come from Jesus, but represent later attempts to explain allegorically for the Church what the parables were supposed to mean. On the principle that each parable is intended to convey one leading truth, these declare the coming or presence of the Kingdom as a process of judgment or selection. The details must not be stressed. The parables may have originally referred to the presence of the Kingdom in Jesus' own time. The harvest had arrived and the catch of fish had been made; men were being sifted and judged there and then, by their attitude towards Jesus' own work.

There are other passages where the Kingdom is not expressly stated to be in the future but this aspect is hinted at. The scribe who was declared to be 'not far from the Kingdom of God' (Mark 12: 34) was nevertheless not yet within it. Jesus spoke of the conditions under which men may or may not 'enter the Kingdom of God' (Mark 9: 47; 10: 15, 23-25). This again suggests a future state. In the parables of growth, on the usual interpretation, there is a climax in the future, when the seed will produce a harvest (Mark 4: 26-29) and the mustard seed will become a great plant (Mark 4: 30-32).

(iii) For Jesus the Kingdom of God was a universal Rule. For the Jews of his day the Kingdom was primarily a national concern. The members were to be those of the chosen race who had faithfully observed the Jewish religious Law. For the Gentiles there was little or no room. Jesus, however, emphasised the non-national and universal nature of the Kingdom. This is implied in his call to those who were outcasts from Judaism — tax-collectors and sinful people — and his willingness to mingle with them. He was also ready to listen to and help the Syro-Phoenician woman (Mark 7: 24-30) and the Roman centurion of Capernaum (Luke 7: 2-9; Matt. 8: 5-13).

In addition to these actions, Jesus also explicitly spoke of the Kingdom as something in which all men might share. Men would come from all the points of the compass, while Jesus' contemporary fellow-countrymen were outside (Luke 13: 28f; Matt. 8: 11f). The Kingdom would be 'taken away' from the Jews and given to 'a nation bringing forth the fruits thereof' (Matt. 21: 43). The Kingdom of God was frequently envisaged among the Jews under the symbol of a Messianic banquet. This explains the exclamation of one of the hearers of Jesus: 'Blessed is he who shall eat bread in the Kingdom of God' (Luke 14: 16). In reply, Jesus told the parable of the Great Supper, with its implication that the guests invited to the banquet — the Jews — were unwilling to accept when the time came and indeed churlishly refused to come, so the outcast and despised people — the Gentiles — were brought in (Luke 14: 16-24; cf. Matt. 22: 1-14). In the parable of the Judgment, the Kingdom is not for those who have observed the Jewish Law but for any among 'all the nations' who have dealt kindly with the King (Matt. 25: 32, 34).

This aspect of the Kingdom, as a universal rule of God, is obviously in the future. It was anticipated in the ministry of Jesus, but could not be fully realised then.

It is probable that we make a mistake if we try to discover some consistent and rigid conception throughout Jesus' teaching on the Kingdom. Surely he spoke of this in many ways. T. W. Manson suggests that it is as pointless to ask whether the Kingdom is essentially present or future as it would be to pose the same question about the Fatherhood of God. Both are eternal. Like God's Fatherhood, the Kingdom is here; whenever men acknowledge God as King, his reign has begun. But its consummation is still in the future, when all men will acknowledge him. So men may realise its presence but still pray: 'Thy Kingdom come' and look and work for the time when the will of God is done on earth as it is already done in the heavenly sphere.

Jesus and the Son of Man

The term Son of Man had a long history behind it before it appeared in our Gospels. In Hebrew and Aramaic the phrase 'a son of man' meant simply 'a man' and it is used in this sense in the Old Testament. In accordance with the parallelism characteristic of Hebrew poetry, the writer of Psalm 8, after asking 'What is man?', adds 'And (what is) the son of man?' (Ps. 8: 4). In Psalm 80: 17 'the man of thy right hand' is paralleled by 'the son of man whom thou madest strong for thyself'. The prophets used the same idiom. In Isaiah 56: 2 'the man that doeth this' is the same as 'the son of man that holdeth fast by it'. (See also Job 16: 21; 25: 6; 35: 8.) Used in the plural, 'sons of men' meant 'human beings' (Ps. 12: 8; 89: 47; Eccles. 3: 21, R.V. margin). In the book of Ezekiel the phrase occurs many times, when the prophet is addressed by Yahweh as 'Son of man'. Here its use may imply that in some capacity Ezekiel was representative of his fellow-men.

A new development started from the use of the name in the book of Daniel. The visionary, writing in the midst of the persecution of the Jews by the Greek Syrian king, Antiochus Epiphanes (168 B.C.), sees, after picturing the great world-empires which in turn have oppressed Israel, 'one like a son of man' coming to God 'with the clouds of heaven' (Dan. 7: 13-14). This means 'a figure like a man' — in contrast to the 'beasts' which represent the earthly empires — and is explained later as being 'the kingdom of the saints of the Most High' (Dan. 7: 18, 22) — that is, Israel. This figure is to reign in triumph, after the temporary victory of the great empires.

This idea was developed in later apocalyptic works. The figure of 'one like a son of man' became personal and was referred to as 'the Son of Man'. He was an 'Elect One', who appeared in connection with visions of the coming new age; he would come with God for the judgment of the world, to condemn the wicked and to reign over the righteous. In the Parables of Enoch (written probably in the first century B.C.) he is called 'the Son of Man', while in Ezra (about A.D. 90) he is referred to as 'The Man', who brings in the Messianic Age.

The term Son of Man is used in the Gospels about eighty times. There are two occasions on which it is used before the acknowledgment of Jesus as Messiah at Caesarea Philippi — in Mark 2: 10 and parallels ('the Son of Man has authority[1] on earth to forgive sins') and Mark 2: 28 ('the Son of Man is lord of the Sabbath'). In each case it has been suggested that, in accordance with Hebrew and Aramaic idiom, the term means simply 'man'. 'Man on earth' has authority to declare sins forgiven and, since 'the Sabbath was made for man' (Mark 2: 27), man has power over the Sabbath. The alternative is to assume that Jesus meant himself, as the Messiah. But this seems too early in the ministry for him to make such a claim and it would have no meaning for his hearers. To forgive sins and to lord it over the Sabbath were not necessarily Messianic functions. The third possibility is that both passages are additions to the original narrative, comments by a Christian preacher or teacher, to impress on his hearers the authority of Jesus as shown in these incidents.

After the incident at Caesarea Philippi Jesus speaks of the Son of Man in two ways:

(i) The Son of Man is one who serves and suffers. Immediately after Peter's acknowledgment, Jesus began to teach that the Son of Man must go to Jerusalem and suffer at the hands of the Sanhedrin. Mark gives this prediction three times (8: 31; 9: 31; 10: 33–34). This was such an unusual and unacceptable thought that Peter began to reprove Jesus for this saying and he received in turn a sharp rebuke (Mark 8: 32–33). The

[1] Both the A.V. and R.V. are incorrect in rendering this as 'power'.

story of the request of James and John for the chief places in Jesus' coming 'glory', which called forth more teaching from Jesus on the necessity of service, ends with the saying: 'Even (or: also) the Son of Man came not to be served but to serve' (Mark 10: 45). To a man who declared that he would follow Jesus wherever he went, he replied that, although animals had their homes, 'the Son of Man has nowhere to lay his head' (Luke 9: 58). He declared that it was written of the Son of Man that he would suffer (Mark 9: 12). As we have seen above (see p. 162), it is probable that Jesus was here thinking of the picture of the suffering Servant as given in Deutero-Isaiah and combining with this the term Son of Man. The same idea probably lies behind the saying in Mark 10: 45, that the Son of Man would 'give his life a ransom for many'.

(ii) In other places Jesus speaks of the future exaltation and triumph of the Son of Man. This is nearer the contemporary and conventional picture of the Son of Man, but Jesus makes this triumph dependent on service and suffering first. The three predictions of the Passion each conclude with a promise that 'after three days he shall rise again'. It is doubtful if Jesus so definitely predicted his resurrection after death, for the disciples were totally unprepared for his appearance when it did take place. The exact phrases used in the Gospels probably reflect rather the assurance of the early Church; yet it is probable that Jesus did conclude the warnings about the fate in store for him at Jerusalem with an assurance that this would not be the end — that his apparent defeat would end in victory. This was to take place 'after three days', which is an eastern way of saying 'in a very short time'.

THE KINGDOM OF GOD AND THE SON OF MAN 175

Elsewhere Jesus speaks of the 'coming' or the 'day' of the Son of Man, as a conception with which his hearers would be familiar. He declared that the attitude of men towards himself would determine their reception by the Son of man, who would be ashamed of them if they were ashamed of Jesus and his words (Mark 8: 38; the Q version is in Luke 12: 8–9 and Matt. 10: 32–33). In some cases the conventional apocalyptic ideas seem to be reproduced. The Son of Man is described as 'coming in clouds with great power and glory' and as sending forth his angels to gather the elect (Mark 13: 24–27). When the High Priest at his trial asked Jesus whether he was the Messiah or not, Mark says that he added to his statement that he was the words: 'You will see the Son of Man sitting at the right hand of power and coming with the clouds of heaven' (Mark 14: 62). There is an obvious reminiscence of Daniel 7: 13 here.

There are three passages in the Gospels in which Jesus speaks at greater length about the coming or day of the Son of Man. One is Mark 13 (reproduced in Luke 21: 5–33 and expanded in Matthew 24). Here are detailed 'signs of the end' — false Messiahs (verses 6, 21–22), wars and calamities (verses 7–8), tribulation (verses 9–13), desecration (verse 14) and unnatural phenomena in the heavens (verses 24–25), before the coming of the Son of Man and the Judgment (verses 26–27). The dominant theme here is the assurance that the present distress is but the beginning of the end (verses 7, 13, 23, 30, 33, 37). The suggestion has already been considered above (see p. 73) that the writer has here made use of an apocalyptic work. Whether this is the case or not, it is probable that some matter not actually taught by Jesus has been included.

But there are genuine sayings as well, words of warning and encouragement to the disciples. Many of these may have been uttered on various occasions but they are here put in an eschatological setting.

The document Q also contained apocalyptic matter — Luke 12: 35-48 and 17: 22-37. Here the emphasis is on the sudden nature of the day of the Son of Man. His coming will be unexpected, like the breaking-in of a thief (Luke 12: 39-40). Men must watch, like servants waiting for the return of their master from a wedding feast (Luke 12: 35-48). The day of the Son of Man comes suddenly like lightning across the sky, like the flood in the time of Noah or like the destruction of Sodom (Luke 17: 23-30). Men must watch, so that they may 'stand before the Son of Man' (Luke 21: 34-36). The Son of Man comes 'in an hour that you think not' (Luke 12: 40).

This teaching about the sudden and unexpected nature of the coming of the Son of Man seems to represent more the mind of Jesus than the detailed apocalyptic 'signs' detailed in Mark 13. Jesus had refused to give any sign to the Pharisees who demanded it, declaring that none was required except 'the sign of Jonah' (Luke 11: 29). This probably means a prophet preaching to the people to whom he was sent, Jonah to his contemporaries and Jesus to his. Similarly Jesus declared that the Kingdom of God did not come 'with observation', in the popular apocalyptic fashion (Luke 17: 20-21).

Thus it seems from these passages that Jesus expected some great event or climax, for which the disciples were to be on the watch. A summary verse in Mark 13: 30 says that 'all these things' were to be accomplished before that generation had passed away. The words to the Sanhedrin — 'you will see the Son of Man . . .' (Mark 14: 62) — also show that something which was going to happen within a few years was thought of.

Jesus and the future consummation

It may seem difficult to obtain any consistent teaching from the passages studied here or to be able to form any definite view of how Jesus conceived the coming of the Kingdom of God or the day of the Son of Man. The early Church seems to have thought that he was referring to himself and spoke of his own future coming in power and glory. This gave rise to the popular view of a Second Advent of Christ (or Parousia, to use the New Testament term for it). The difficulty of this view is that Jesus never speaks of a 'return' of *himself* and never speaks of the Son of Man as coming *again* — only of his 'coming' or 'day'. A further objection is that Jesus spoke of this as happening within the lifetime of his hearers. There would be no point in telling the disciples to be on the watch for an event which was not to happen for centuries afterwards!

It is indeed possible to hold, as Schweitzer emphasised, that Jesus expected his own return as the Son of Man upon the clouds of heaven; our conclusion in this case must be that he was mistaken, that this expectation shared the disappointment which the hope of the immediate manifestation of the Kingdom of God suffered. Some have sought to avoid this conclusion by suggesting that Jesus was using conventional current terms in a figurative or spiritual way and was speaking of the final triumph of Christianity in the world.

C. H. Dodd suggests that Jesus spoke of his ultimate triumph in different ways. Sometimes he spoke of it as 'resurrection after three days'; at other times he referred to the 'day of the Son of Man' and sometimes to his 'coming on the clouds of heaven'. All three expressions are representations of the same idea. In connection with the first prediction of the Passion by Jesus, there are three expressions which may be intended as variants of the same thought. The Son of Man 'will rise again' after three days (Mark 9: 31); he will 'come in the glory of his Father' (8: 38) and the disciples will 'see the Kingdom of God come with power' (9: 1). These are different ways of saying that he will be triumphant, but it will be a triumph not such as an earthly monarch would enjoy; it will be realised in the life and in the hearts of the disciples themselves. Then the Kingdom of God will be truly 'in the midst of men'.

BOOKS FOR FURTHER READING AND STUDY

THERE is a vast literature on the composition and contents of the Gospels. The books listed here are those which have fairly recently appeared and deal more specifically with the subject-matter of this book. Books which deal with the Greek text of the Gospels have been omitted.

The composition and characteristics of the Gospels:
- A. Barr: *A Diagram of Synoptic Relations.*
- A. Huck: *Gospel Parallels.*
- B. H. Streeter: *The Four Gospels.*
- R. V. G. Tasker: *The Nature and Purpose of the Gospels.*

The Life of Christ:
- C. J. Cadoux: *The Life of Jesus.*
- C. J. Cadoux: *The Historic Mission of Jesus.*
- H. A. Guy: *The Life of Christ: Notes on Passages in the Gospels.*
- V. Taylor: *The Life and Ministry of Jesus.*
- B. L. Wolff: *The Background and Beginnings of the Gospel Story.*

The teaching of Jesus:
- C. H. Dodd: *The Parables of the Kingdom.*
- J. Jeremias: *The Parables of Jesus.*
- A. M. Hunter: *The Words and Work of Jesus.*

H. Martin: *The Parables of the Gospels.*
T. W. Manson: *The Sayings of Jesus.*
T. W. Manson: *The Teaching of Jesus.*
T. W. Manson: *The Servant Messiah.*
A. Schweitzer: *The Mystery of the Kingdom of God.*
B. T. D. Smith: *The Parables of the Synoptic Gospels.*

Form Criticism:

M. Dibelius: *From Tradition to Gospel.*
B. S. Easton: *The Gospel before the Gospels.*
E. B. Redlich: *Form Criticism.*
V. Taylor: *The Formation of the Gospel Tradition.*

Books on separate Gospels:

B. W. Bacon: *The Gospel of Mark.*
P. Carrington: *The Primitive Christian Calendar.*
A. Farrer: *A Study in St. Mark.*
H. A. Guy: *The Origin of the Gospel of Mark.*
R. H. Lightfoot: *The Gospel Message of St. Mark.*
A. E. J. Rawlinson: *The Gospel according to St. Mark.*
G. D. Kilpatrick: *The Origins of the Gospel according to St. Matthew.*
H. J. Cadbury: *The Making of Luke–Acts.*
A. R. C. Leaney: *The Gospel according to St. Luke.*
V. Taylor: *Behind the Third Gospel.*
The Clarendon Bible volumes: Mark (Blunt), Matthew (Green), Luke (Balmforth).
The Moffatt New Testament Commentary volumes: Mark (Branscomb), Matthew (Robinson), Luke (Manson).
The Torch Commentary volumes: Mark (Hunter), Matthew (Cox), Luke (Browning).
The Penguin Gospels: Mark (Nineham), Matthew (Felton), Luke (Caird), John (Marsh).

INDEX OF SUBJECTS

Aphorisms, 99f
Apocalypse, Little, 73f, 175
Authority of Jesus, 34f

Baptism of Jesus, 157, 160, 161
Barriers between men, 141ff
Beatitudes, 138
Beelzebub, 35, 39
Biographical stories, 7
Birth of Jesus, 25f

Caesarea Philippi, 29, 173
Character of Jesus, 136f
Christ—*see* Messiah
Consummation of the age, 114, 175ff
Covenant, 31
Criticism, 5

Eschatology in the Gospels, 73, 113f, 165ff, 174ff
Essenes, 23

Forgiveness, 139, 143f
Form Criticism, 4ff, 67
Four-document hypothesis, 96

Galilee, Jesus' work in, 27f, 34ff
Gentiles, 29, 142f, 170f
God:
  as Father, 152f
  Jewish idea of God, 151f
  Kingdom of God, 164ff
  Son of God, 154, 159ff
Gospel, 1ff

Healing acts of Jesus, 27f
Herods, 16ff

Ideal character, 136
Individual, Jesus and the, 136ff

Jericho, 30
Jerusalem:
  journey to, 29f
  Jesus in, 30ff, 40ff
  destruction of, 12, 41
Jewish religion, 36ff
John Mark, 75f

Kingdom of God, 164ff

L material, 92ff
Last Supper, 31, 101
Law (Jewish), 35ff, 139
Little Apocalypse, 73f, 175
Luke, Gospel of:
  authorship, 130ff
  characteristics, 128ff
  construction, 123ff
  date, 132ff
  peculiar matter, 92ff

M material, 90ff
Man, Jesus' teaching about, 135ff

INDEX OF SUBJECTS

Mark, Gospel of:
 authorship, 74ff
 characteristics, 63f
 conclusion, 79ff
 date, 76ff
 Mark and Q, 89f
 peculiar matter, 60f
 priority of Mark, 52ff
 sources, 70ff
 theology, 68ff
Markan outline, 62, 65f
Matthew, Gospel of:
 authorship, 115ff
 characteristics, 111ff
 construction, 110f
 date, 120ff
 peculiar matter, 90ff
Messiah in the Synoptics, 157ff
Messianic ideas, 154ff
Miracles of Jesus, 27f
Miracle stories, 6f
'My brother', 141ff
'Myself', 136ff

Nazareth, 35
Non-Markan parallels, 82ff

Old Testament history, 14f
Opposition to Jesus, 34ff, 40ff
Oral hypothesis, 48f
Oral tradition, 1ff

Palestine:
 map, 17
 situation in, 15ff
Papias on Mark, 71
Papias on Matthew, 117f
Parables, 106ff
Paradigms, 5f
Parousia, 114, 175ff

Passion story, 30ff
Peter and Mark, 71ff
Pharisees, 21, 34ff
Phoenicia, 29
Pictorial language, 100f
Poetry, 101ff
Political situation, 15ff
Pontius Pilate, 32, 42
Priests, 40ff
Pronouncement stories, 5f
Proto-Luke, 124ff
Publicans, 36, 142

Q:
 contents, 84ff
 order and language, 87f
 and Mark, 89f

Realised eschatology, 167
Reconciliation, 143ff
Resurrection appearances, 33
Riches, 146ff
Romans, 15f, 143, 149

Sabbath observance, 38f
Sadducees, 22
Samaria and Samaritans, 18, 30, 142
Sanhedrin, 32, 41f
Scribes, 23, 34ff
Servant of God, 161f
Service, 145ff
Sin, 138f
'Sinners', 35f
Social relations, 141ff
Son of God, 154, 159ff
Son of man, 162, 171ff
State and politics, 148f
Synagogue, 19
'Synoptic', 25

INDEX OF SUBJECTS

Synoptic outline, 25ff
Synoptic problem, 43ff

Tax-collectors, 36, 142
Teaching methods, 98ff
Temple, 20, 40
Temptation of Jesus, 157
Testimonies, books of, 119
Traditions of the elders, 21, 37
Trial of Jesus, 32, 41f

Urmarkus, 61

Verbal inspiration, 47f

Wealth, 146ff
Worship, Jewish, 19f

Zealots, 23